Stop Orders

A practical guide to using stop orders for
traders and investors

by Tony Loton

HARRIMAN HOUSE LTD
3A Penns Road
Petersfield
Hampshire
GU32 2EW
GREAT BRITAIN

Tel: +44 (0)1730 233870
Fax: +44 (0)1730 233880
Email: enquiries@harriman-house.com
Website: www.harriman-house.com

First edition published in Great Britain in 2009 by Harriman House.

Copyright © Harriman House Ltd

The right of Tony Loton to be identified as the author has been asserted
in accordance with the Copyright, Design and Patents Act 1988.

978-1-906659-28-8

British Library Cataloguing in Publication Data
A CIP catalogue record for this book can be obtained from the British Library.

Printed and bound by Lightning Source

Contents

About the Author

Tony Loton trades a range of financial instruments including equities, exchange traded funds, covered warrants, and spread bets on his own account. He would describe himself as a graduate of the Investment School of Hard Knocks.

Tony has written regularly for the Barclays Stockbrokers *Smart Investor* magazine and has previously written and published financial titles including *Don't Lose Money! (in the Stock Markets)*, *Financial Trading Patterns*, and *Stock Fundamentals On Trial: Do Dividend Yield, P/E and PEG Really Work?*

In October 2008, Tony was featured as a day trader in the money section of the UK's *Sunday Times*.

You can find out more about Tony Loton's trading and investment books at **www.lotontech.com/money** and read his blog at **http://lotontech-money.blogspot.com**.

Acknowledgements

Writing a book like this one is a lonely business; a fact that is compounded by the subject matter (trading) being itself a lonely activity. Nevertheless, a book project is usually the work of more than one person – so I can't take all the credit.

I'd like to thank Louise Hinchen of Harriman House for contacting me in the first place with the suggestion of working together, Suzanne Anderson for organising the commercial aspects with utmost efficiency, and Stephen Eckett for his editorial support and constructive criticism.

Special thanks go to Nick McDonald (of *tradewithprecision.com*) and Mike Baghdady (of *spyglasstrading.co.uk*) for their contributions to Chapter 14, and to Richard Powell (of *presswire.com*) for sourcing those contributions. Special thanks also go to Malcolm Pryor (of *spreadbettingcentral.co.uk*) for his contribution to Chapter 14.

Finally I'd like to thank my wife Debbie for her help with my other publishing adventures, and my children – Becky and Matt – for just being good kids (most of the time).

Foreword

It was awe-inspiring to learn that an author was writing a book on the subject of Stops. In my 32 years of trading I do not recall ever having come across a book dedicated solely to this subject. I wish I had!

Stops are, without doubt, one of the most important aspects of successful trading. But, generally, trading and technical analysis books cover this most important topic in a rather casual manner.

A common misconception is that successful trading is about making money, but there is nothing further from the truth. Trading is a business of risk. Traders assume and trade risk in order to become successful in their trading and eventually make a profit. Key to this is to first learn how to control and manage risk – the number one responsibility of any successful trader and the only aspect of trading that is ever fully under their control.

The way to control risk is through the correct use of Stops.

Mike Baghdady. A veteran of the NYBOT trading floor and global financial market and the world's foremost expert on Price Behaviour.

Preface

What the book covers

This book covers the most important weapon in the armoury of any trader, investor or spread bettor: the *stop order*.

The techniques described in this book are theoretically applicable to a wide range of tradable securities and financial instruments including equities, exchange traded funds, currencies, commodities, options, contracts for difference and spread bets. Throughout the book I use the terms *securities* and *financial instruments* somewhat interchangeably to refer to any of those markets.

Anything that is tradable at a price determined by the market *could*, broker permitting, have a stop order applied to it. In practice you will find that some brokers might limit the range of tradable instruments to which stop orders may be applied, and you'll read more about this later.

My own inclination towards equity and index trading will be evident in the examples, but to show the wide applicability of stop orders I have included examples of commodity and foreign exchange trades. You will also find some additional contributions from currency traders in Chapter 14.

Who this book is for

This book is for investors, traders, and spread bettors.

Investors

Where I refer to investors I am talking primarily about those who place money with a fund manager for the long term or who manage their own investments.

Although many funds do not lend themselves to the application of stop orders, because they are not priced and traded continually throughout the day, the idea of noting stop levels mentally, or on paper, and then executing these stop orders manually (by instructing the fund manager to sell) may be a valid strategy.

What about buy-and-holders?

As a diehard buy-and-hold investor you might be tempted to put this book down right now! After all, a stop-based buy-and-hold strategy is an oxymoron, isn't it? Actually, I don't think so. As a *position trader*, my ideal holding period would be forever, but I won't do so unconditionally. In most cases I would intend to hold a position as long as possible – but no longer.

What about value investors?

Unlike technical traders, fundamentals-driven value investors are concerned with a wider range of characteristics than mere price action. But they ignore price action at their peril. Even value investors should be minded to limit their losses using stop orders, as protection against those cases where their value judgments prove to be incorrect as reflected by the price action.

Traders

Where I refer to traders I am talking primarily about non-professionals who trade actively, usually long (hope for a rising price) but sometimes short (hope for a falling price). Your trading timescale will be medium to long term, but you may have experimented with short-term day trading.

The term trader may also refer to professional traders who trade a range of financial instruments, including foreign exchange, commodities, and more exotic instruments. Professional traders will have direct market access and much-reduced transaction costs, and from a retail (non-professional) point of view will have more in common with...

Spread Bettors

Where I refer to spread bettors I am talking about private, non-professional (but by no means amateur) traders in the UK or Europe (not the USA) who trade derivative financial instruments at low cost and tax-free, both long and short, over any timescale via a spread betting account.

Spread bettors may be day traders, swing traders, position traders, or (I'll argue) investors. I present spread bettors as a separate class of market participants because spread betting opens up possibilities to individual traders that were hitherto only available to professional traders, namely:

- The ability to trade long or short with equal ease.
- The ability to trade without transaction charges (other than the bid-ask spread).
- The ability to trade tax-free (currently, in the UK at least).
- Easy access to a range of range of markets, including currencies and commodities.

Some, but by no means all, of the strategies described in this book may be applied more effectively via a spread betting account than via a regular equity brokerage account. Some spread betting providers may require a mandatory initial *stop-loss order* on any position that you open, and in a limited risk spread betting account these mandatory stop-loss orders may even be *guaranteed* to close out your position for an assured maximum loss.

Whether you describe yourself as a trader, an investor, or a spread bettor, you should regard the *stop order* as an essential tool in your armoury.

How this book is structured

Part 1 of this book (Stop Orders in Theory) represents a compendium of the types of stop orders that exist. This part of the book acts as an introduction for novices, and as a handy reference for the more experienced traders, investors, and spread bettors who find themselves temporarily at a loss trying to remember – for example – which problem is solved by a *stop-with-limit order*. This part may be read sequentially or by dipping in to the chapters that interest you; and as such any repetition between the chapters is both intentional and necessary. You can think of this part of the book as describing the *tools* of the trade.

Part 2 (Stop Orders in Practice) offers a more hands-on coverage of the use of stop orders in real-life scenarios under real market conditions, illustrated with price charts for stock indices, individual stocks, commodities, and foreign exchange currency pairs. If you think of Part 1 as describing the *tools* at your disposal, you can think of Part 2 as describing real-life *techniques* for using those tools.

If this was a motor vehicle manual, Part 1 would tell you what the various controls do and Part 2 would teach you how to become a better driver. Experienced drivers may wish to cut to the chase by skipping forward to Part 2. You can always return to Part 1 for reference later.

Part One: Stop Orders in Theory (the Tools)

Chapter 1 – Orders, Stop Orders and their Many Flavours

Introduces market orders, limit orders, the various kinds of stop orders and their attributes such as guaranteed and good until. Distinguishes between long traders and short traders and their corresponding interpretations of stop order terminology.

Chapter 2 – Stop Order to Sell

An introduction to the *stop order to sell* as a mechanism for cutting a loss or securing a profit on a long position, or for entering a short position in line with the falling trend.

Chapter 3 – Stop Order to Buy

An introduction to the *stop order to buy* as a mechanism for entering a long trade in line with the rising trend, or for cutting a loss or securing a profit on a short trade.

Chapter 4 – Trailing Stop Order to Sell

An introduction to the *trailing stop order to sell* as a mechanism for exiting a long position at the end of an uptrend, or for entering a short position at the start of a downtrend.

Chapter 5 – Trailing Stop Order to Buy

An introduction to the *trailing stop order to buy* as a mechanism for entering a long position at the start of an uptrend, or for exiting a short position at the end of a downtrend.

Chapter 6 – Guaranteed Stop, and Stop with Limit

An introduction to *guaranteed stops* and *stops-with-limits* as mitigation against price gaps.

Chapter 7 – Combining Stop Orders

An introduction to the use of stop orders (and limit orders) in combination to achieve trading objectives such as buy low sell high.

Part Two: Stop Orders in Practice (the Techniques)

Chapter 8 – Trading Timescales

A discussion of how the use of stop orders applies to various trading styles from short-term day trading through to long-term investing.

Chapter 9 – Price Gaps and Whipsaw Losses

An practical examination of price gaps (the bane of stop orders) and the associated issues of over-trading and whipsaw losses.

Chapter 10 – Stop Placement

Practical guidance on where (how tight or how wide) to place stop orders.

Chapter 11 – Position Sizing

How to manage risk using the alternative yet complementary technique of position sizing, and discussion of the important interplay between stop placement and position sizing.

Chapter 12 – Perfect Trades

A series of trades illustrating the successful use of stop orders under real market conditions.

Chapter 13 – Imperfect Trades

A series of trades illustrating how the use of stop orders could prove to be less effective under real market conditions, with recommendations on how those trades could have been improved.

Chapter 14 – When to Hold and When to Fold

What parallels can be drawn between trading and games of chance such as Poker? How do experienced traders make profits by practising sound money management: knowing when to hold and when to fold?

Chapter 15 – Top Tips for using Stop Orders

All of the key tips that are implicit in Part 2 of the book – in one handy list!

Chapter 16 – Conclusion: The Case For and Against Stop Orders

Are stop orders for everyone? I think so, but not everyone agrees.

Terminology

Traders and investors will operate in the market either by direct market access or via an intermediary such as a stockbroker (not necessarily restricted to trading stocks) or a spread betting provider. Where that distinction is important to the way stop orders work – or are not allowed at all, for example, where the intermediary is a mutual fund manager – I will use the appropriate term for the intermediary. Where the distinction is not so important, I will use the shorthand term 'broker' to refer to any of those intermediaries.

Where it is important for me to distinguish between traders and investors, or between traders and the specific subset of traders who operate through a spread betting account, I will do so. Where the distinction is not so important, the generic term *trader* will suffice.

Assumptions

This book is aimed at a wide readership, from amateur investors to professional traders, and therefore some level of prior knowledge has to be assumed. It is assumed that the reader has done sufficient prior reading so as to have an understanding of – or the ability to quickly grasp – common trading concepts such as price support and resistance levels.

Charts

In Part 1, the charts are stylised charts that show how the use of a particular kind of stop order is meant to play out, or not.

In Part 2, real charts have been generated using real market data.

Introduction

As a self-taught trader and investor – a graduate of what I call the *Investment School of Hard Knocks* – I spent many years figuring out a lot of things for myself using a combination of broker-supplied educational material and mutually-conflicting books. One of the things I had to figure out was how, and when, to apply what I now consider to be the most important tool in the trader's armoury: the **stop order**.

At first glance it seems so simple. A stop order allows you to *stop a loss*, which in trading circles is generally acknowledged to be a good thing – some traders even calling it the *most* important thing. But there's more to it than that, because successful traders use stop orders in a variety of different ways in addition to their role as a stop-loss mechanism:

- They use stop orders to enter new positions as well as to exit existing (bad) positions.

- They use stop orders to secure a profit, without prematurely crystallising the profit by closing a trade.

- They use stop orders to sell short and then buy long, so as to benefit from falling prices.

- They use (trailing) stop orders to track a falling price, so as to *buy* at a low price when the trend begins to turn up.

- They use (trailing) stop orders to track a rising price, so as to *sell* at a high price when the trend begins to turn down.

- They use stop orders to partially automate their trading, in order to be able to leave their computer screens long enough to make a cup of tea (for the day traders) or go on holiday (for the longer term traders and investors).

In this book about stop orders we need to consider all of those possibilities, and in doing so we find that the humble stop order is not so humble after all.

Taking the Emotion out of Trading

I've heard it said about golf that the good players are not necessarily the ones who hit the best shots, but the ones who hit the least number of bad shots. The same may be true of trading and investing. You might get lucky by taking a few wild adrenalin-filled swings, but you are just as likely to find yourself perpetually in the financial long grass.

What you really need in both games is *consistency*.

Stop orders help you to trade consistently because they allow you to specify – in advance, with a cool head – a price at which it will make sense for you to buy or sell regardless of your emotional state at the time that your target price is reached. When the time comes, your stop order with the broker will (or at least should) be carried out without question. This is a good thing because 'when the time comes' is often the worst time for you to make a rational trading decision. When all about you are losing their heads – due to fear and greed – the stop order will ensure that you don't lose yours.

Why buy or sell at a less favourable price?

One thing that bothered me about stop orders upon first encountering them was that the fact that, as one of my spread betting providers puts it:

> *A stop order is an order that executes at a price less favourable than the current market price.*

Whereas a **limit order** allows you to buy at a more favourable (lower) price than the current market price, or to sell at a more favourable (higher) price than the current market price, a **stop order** encourages you to do exactly the opposite!

That sounds rather odd doesn't it?

Why would anyone ever want to buy or sell at a less favourable price than the current market price? In this book I will show you why.

Part One

Stop Orders in Theory
(the Tools)

1

Orders, Stop Orders and their Many Flavours

If you've researched stop orders already on your broker's website you may well have encountered phrases like –

stop order to buy

stop order to sell

trailing stop

guaranteed stop

stop-with-limit

You might also have encountered the notion of a stop order being *good until*. In this chapter I'll define those terms – the many flavours of stop orders – and the relationships between them.

Note that here and in the other chapters of this part of the book, I use the term "many flavours of stop orders" to mean the stop order mechanisms (or order types) and their parameters that may be offered by your broker or spread betting provider. These are the tools of the trade. In some books you will see stops categorised as per cent retracement stops, volatility stops, support and resistance stops, and so on, according to the levels at which those stops are set relative to the current market price. These are stop placement techniques, which I defer to Part 2 of this book. On your broker's website you are likely to see a button inviting you to place a *trailing stop order to sell*, but you are most unlikely to see a button inviting you to place a *volatility stop*.

Before we look specifically at stop orders, I should first introduce – or remind you – of basic market orders.

A Brief Introduction to Order Types

Orders that you can give a broker fall broadly into two categories:

1. *Market orders* that are intended to trade more-or-less immediately and unconditionally at the current or next available market price.

2. *Limit orders* and *stop orders* that are intended to sit with your broker as standing orders to be executed when a certain condition is met (i.e. when the price reaches a price you set).

I'll set the scene by introducing market orders and limit orders in the two sections that follow; with stop orders – of course – being the subject of the rest of the book.

Market Orders

A market order could take the form of an *at best* order in which you instruct a broker to buy the specified security as soon as possible at the best possible price. The order should be executed immediately, or in the very near future, but you cannot be certain at what price.

Alternatively, a market order could take the form of a *quote and deal* order in which the broker quotes a price by telephone or on your computer screen during market hours and you have a few seconds or minutes to accept the trade at the quoted price.

The point about these orders is that they are more like immediate instructions than standing orders, and are designed to trade unconditionally at or around the current market price. In the case of an *at best* order placed out of hours, the current market price will mean the next day's opening price.

Limit Orders

Limit orders are designed to execute sometime in the future (which could be immediately) if a certain condition is met.

- For an order to **buy,** this would usually mean to buy at a price *no greater* than the limit you had set.

- For an order to **sell,** it would usually mean to sell at a price *no lower* than the limit you had set.

Thus, a limit order ensures that you trade at what you think is a good price, or not at all.

For example, suppose you want to buy some shares at a price no more than $0.80 per share. The limit order should execute immediately if the current price is $0.70. If the current price is $0.90 per share, the order will be put on hold until the price reaches the limit you set. The price may never reach your limit, which is why limit orders are said to "not guarantee execution".

Suppose you want to sell your shares at a price of at least $1.20 per share. The limit order should execute immediately if the current price is $1.30. If the current price is $1.10 per share, the order will be put on hold until the price reaches the limit you set. Once again, limit orders "do not guarantee execution".

One way to use limit orders is for buying low and selling high in a range bound market. Suppose the FTSE 100 has been oscillating between 5000 and 5500. You might place a limit order to buy at no more than 5100; and once bought, you might place a limit order to sell you out at no less than 5400. In this pattern you would be aiming to capture a profit of at least 300 points in every cycle.

> **!** A **limit order to buy** always *triggers from above*, when the price falls to the limit you set.
>
> A **limit order to sell** always *triggers from below*, when the price rises to the limit you set.

The Limits of Limit Orders

Do you see the problem with this limit buy/sell pattern?

It works only as long as the index or other financial instrument trades within the expected range. In my example, if there is a fall below 5000 (the support level) or a breakout above 5500 (the resistance level) you will be buying into a falling market or selling out of a rising market. Ideally, what you'd like to do is buy into a rising market and sell out of a falling market; which is where stop orders come in.

In this book's introduction I highlighted the importance of having an exit strategy. One such strategy is to exit when a particular profit target is reached, and a limit order will allow you to do just that. But the problem with profit targets is that by selling out for a 20% profit you take yourself out of the running for a 100% profit – or more. Whereas **limit orders** serve to *limit your profits* in this way, **stop orders** allow you to *let your profits run*.

Stop Orders and Their Many Flavours

Whereas limit orders, by design, buy you in to a falling market and sell you out of a rising market, stop orders do exactly the opposite: they buy you in to a rising market and sell you out of a falling market.

Without wishing to complicate matters too much at this point, the phrasing would be slightly different for short traders. A stop order would sell them 'in to' a falling market and buy them 'out of' a rising market.

In the brief explanations that follow I use concise names, like **stop order to buy** and **trailing stop order to sell,** so as to distinguish the various flavours. Your broker might use names explicitly like this in order to differentiate the various order types that it provides. Or it might present you with what is apparently a smaller range of stop order types: for example a *stop sell* (or *sell stop*) order type furnished with an onscreen checkbox that transforms it into a *trailing stop sell* order. Your spread betting provider might present you with a single input box labelled *STOP*, which takes on the role of a *stop sell* or *stop buy* according to whether you are applying the order to a long position or a short position. In a nutshell, the provider of your trading platform may well offer you the full set of stop orders presented in this chapter, in the guise of a smaller set of order types.

Stop Order to Sell

A **stop order to sell** is designed to execute sometime in the future when the price of the stock or other security falls to a level that you set. This use of a stop order as *stop loss order* is the most common use, which is why I introduce the *sell* case first.

A **stop order to sell** is often used by long traders and investors as an *exit mechanism*.

> As you will see later, short traders would use a **stop order to sell** as an entry mechanism rather than an exit mechanism.

You may find it enlightening to compare the following statement about the **stop order to sell** with the earlier statement for a limit order to sell.

> **!** A **stop order to sell** always *triggers from above*, when the price falls to the level you set.

vs.

> **!** A **limit order to sell** always *triggers from below*, when the price rises to the limit you set.

Stop Order to Buy

A **stop order to buy** is designed to execute sometime in the future when the price of the stock or other security rises to a level that you set.

A **stop order to buy** is often used by (long) trend followers as an *entry mechanism*.

> As you will see later, short traders would use a **stop order to buy** as an exit mechanism rather than an entry mechanism.

You may find it enlightening to compare the following statement about the **stop order to buy** with the earlier statement for a **limit order to buy.**

> **!** A **stop order to buy** always *triggers from below*, when the price rises to the level you set.

vs.

> **!** A **limit order to buy** always *triggers from above*, when the price falls to the limit you set.

Trailing Stop Order to Sell

A **trailing stop order to sell** is designed to execute sometime in the future when the price of the stock or other security falls from any price peak by an amount that you set.

A stop order may be trailed manually (i.e. you adjust it periodically yourself), or your broker may allow you to specify a stop order that automatically trails at a fixed distance below a rising price.

A **trailing stop order to sell** is often used by long trend followers as an *exit mechanism*, to exit a position when the upward price trend reverses.

> As you will see later, short traders would use a **trailing stop order to sell** as an entry mechanism rather than an exit mechanism.

Trailing Stop Order to Buy

A **trailing stop order to buy** is designed to execute sometime in the future when the price of the stock or other security rises from a price trough by an amount that you set.

Again, this may be a manually-trailed stop order or an order provided by your broker that trails automatically at a fixed distance above a falling price.

A **trailing stop order to buy** could be used by long-trading 'bottom fishers' as an *entry mechanism*; a means of *buying low*.

> As you will see later, short traders would use a **trailing stop order to buy** as an exit mechanism rather than an entry mechanism.

Guaranteed Stop

You might see that your broker describes a stop order as "guaranteeing execution but not price". It means that if your stop level is breached, your position will certainly be closed – or opened, as appropriate – but not necessarily at the price you set. When markets gap (described in Chapter 6 and Chapter 9) you could find that your stop order executes at an unfavourable price.

To alleviate this problem, some brokers and spread betting providers provide a **guaranteed stop** facility. For a nominal additional premium – nothing in life is free, after all – you can be assured that your stop order will execute at exactly the price you set.

Depending on the broker, a guarantee may be applicable to a **stop order to buy**, a **stop order to sell**, and maybe even their *trailing* variants.

Stop with Limit

Some brokers do not provide guaranteed stops, but they do provide another facility to help alleviate the market gapping problem – the **stop with limit**.

The idea is that you can specify a stop order along these lines:

Sell out if the price falls to 100 but not if it gaps down to 80.

Depending on your viewpoint, this facility might be very useful (because it protects you from gaps that might reverse immediately) or very dangerous (because in some cases it may be better to sell out at an unfavourable price rather than not sell out at all).

Depending on the broker, a limit may be applicable to a **stop order to buy**, a **stop order to sell**, and maybe even their *trailing* variants.

Good Until

When you apply a stop order, you can often specify the length of time for which the order is valid.

Your broker might allow you to specify that a stop order is valid for a number of business days, for example from 1 to 30 days. Or your spread betting provider might allow you to specify that a stop order is valid until cancelled, or for one day only. The latter would be of particular interest to a pure day trader who does not wish to open a position automatically at the next day's opening price.

One Cancels Other (OCO)

A **one cancels other** (OCO) order allows you to place two orders, with the execution of one of those orders triggering the cancellation of the other order.

For example, you might conclude that a price oscillating within a very tight trading range will soon break out into a sustained uptrend or downtrend. So as to benefit in either case, you might place simultaneously a **stop order to buy** to trigger if the price breaks out above the resistance level and a **stop order to sell** to trigger if the price breaks out below the support level. If the price breaks upwards your stop order to sell would be redundant, and if the price breaks downwards your stop order to buy would be redundant, so it would make sense for these orders to be **one cancels other**.

Note that not all brokers providers allow OCO orders, and you may be charged a fee.

Why "Many Flavours" of Stop Orders?

You may wonder why I refer to the many *flavours* of stop orders, rather than the many *types*. It's because, as described above:

- There are two basic kinds of stop orders – **stop order to buy**, and its mirror **stop order to sell** – each of which may have a corresponding *trailing* version.

- It may be possible to guarantee the price at which a stop order executes, and you may be able to set a *limit* on the price at which the order executes.

- Finally, you may be able to set a *good until* time period over which the order is valid, and you may be able to combine stop orders such that one cancels another.

These variations on the basic stop order theme are what I refer to as *the many flavours of stop orders*.

Example Order Forms

If you trade online rather than over the phone, your broker or spread betting provider will present some kind of web form via which you can choose your stop order type and specify the required parameters. They may offer a separate form for each of the stop order flavours that I have presented, or a single form that caters for all of the flavours, or anything in between. Two examples follow.

Example Stockbroker Stop Order Form

Figure 1 shows an example stop order form that might appear on a stockbroker's trading platform. In this example you choose the stock to which the stop order is to be applied, the type of stop order (Stop or Trailing Stop) and the type of transaction (Buy, Sell, or Sell All).

Figure 1: Stockbroker Stop Order Form, Step #1

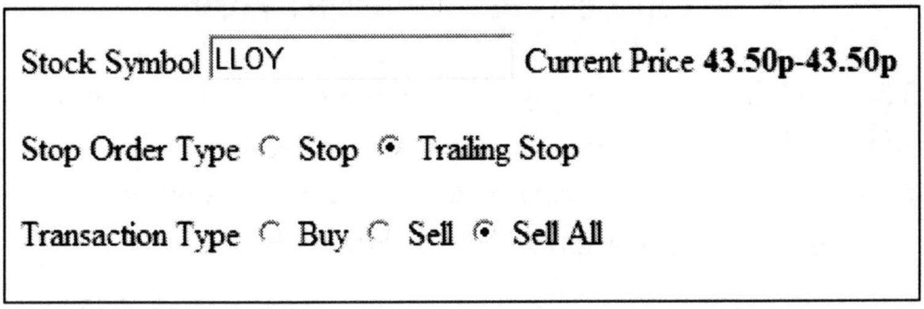

```
Stock Symbol |LLOY              Current Price 43.50p-43.50p

Stop Order Type ⌒ Stop  ⦿ Trailing Stop

Transaction Type ⌒ Buy  ⌒ Sell  ⦿ Sell All
```

My illustrated selections in this step would lead to a subsequent form shown in Figure 2. In this example you would choose the trailing stop distance (in this case 5), the optional limit (in this case 10), and a period for which the order is good (in this case 30 business days).

Figure 2: Stockbroker Stop Order Form, Step #2

SELL ALL of LLOYDS BANKING GP

Current Price **43.50p-43.50p**

Sell when the share price **falls a minimum of** 5

Do not sell if the share price **has fallen more than** 10

To expire in 30 business days.

Example Spread Betting Stop Order Form

The order form provided by your stockbroker may well be much simpler than the previous example, as might your spread betting provider's order form. Figure 3 shows an example stop order form that might appear on a spread betting firm's web page.

In this case trailing stops are not allowed, and the platform knows that this should be a sell order because it is being applied to a long position. Therefore you need only specify your desired stop level (50 in this case) and the period for which the order is good until (Cancelled in this case). This order form allows you to guarantee the stop level by checking the relevant box.

Figure 3: Spread Betting Stop Order Form

Barclays (GBP) Rolling Spread

Type: Amend closing order

Sell **68.43** Buy **68.67**

Stoploss 50　　　　Quantity 1　　　　Guaranteed ☑

Good until ○ End of day ● Cancelled

The Long and Short of Stop Orders

Before we get into the meat of this book, I'd like to reiterate and clarify what I have hinted at with respect to *short* traders.

This part of the book focuses mainly on *long* traders, who benefit when a price rises. But for every use of a stop order by a long trader, there is a possible inverse use of the same stop order by a *short* trader.

In most cases I will describe the long trading or investing case, followed by a brief paragraph in the side note style (example below) that clarifies the short trading case.

Most times, the words 'buy' and 'sell', and 'in' and 'out' – or 'enter' and 'exit' – will be reversed. So where a *long* trader would use a **stop order to sell** so as to limit a potential loss, a *short* trader would use a **stop order to buy** for the same effect. And where a *long* trader would use a **stop order to buy** so as to 'buy in' (or *enter*) a position, a *short* trader would use a **stop order to buy** in order to 'buy out' (or *exit* a position).

If you're committed to long trading and investing only, you need not worry about the additional notes for short traders. If you're an existing or aspiring short trader, the additional notes should make sense without you having to think too deeply about them. My advice: don't even consider short trading until they do!

The acid test would be to come back to this chapter and compare your understanding against this handy table:

Summary of stop orders for long and short trades

	Long Trader or Investor	Short Trader
Stop Order to Sell	EXIT mechanism Sells you out of a falling price trend.	ENTRY mechanism Sells you into a falling price trend.
Stop Order to Buy	ENTRY mechanism Buys you in to a rising price trend.	EXIT mechanism Buys you out of a rising price trend.
Trailing Stop Order to Sell	EXIT mechanism Sells you out when a previously rising trend turns down.	ENTRY mechanism Sells you in when a previously rising trend turns down.
Trailing Stop Order to Buy	ENTRY mechanism Buys you in when a previously falling trend turns up.	EXIT mechanism Buys you out when a previously falling trend turns up.

Note: Wherever I used the phrase 'short trading' I mean something quite different from 'short term trading'. A 'short *term* trader' – who may be a day trader or a swing trader – trades long or short but over a short timescale; whereas a 'short trader' simply bets on a falling price.

A note about Dealing Charges and the Bid–Ask Spread

In the examples that follow, I largely ignore the effect of dealing charges. I do this for simplicity, and because the impact of those dealing charges can vary enormously depending on the broker you choose, the trading platform, and the jurisdiction (i.e. country) you operate in. The drag effect of transaction charges will be very different for a retail investor attempting to day-trade (perhaps unwisely) in a regular brokerage account compared to a position-trading spread bettor compared to a fund manager making multi-million-dollar portfolio adjustments.

But make no mistake. As you will see in Part 2, dealing charges can have a significant effect on your overall performance if you trade often, and so you should keep this in mind. Dealing charges do not usually apply to spread bets.

I have also largely ignored the bid-ask spread (the difference between buying and selling prices) in order to keep the examples simple, and because these will vary according to your chosen stockbroker or spread betting provider, and also according to the specific security you are trading. The effect of the bid-ask spread is implicit in my examples, to the extent that a buy at 5550 with a stop loss order at 5540 would already be halfway to the stop level if there was a 5-point bid-ask spread. Beware those securities that have a wide bid-ask spread relative to your stop distances.

While I have largely ignored these costs-of-trading until Part 2 of this book, you should keep them in mind at all times. Each trade will cost you some money regardless of whether it is a winning or losing trade, and the only way to counter this constant drag on your trading capital is to ensure that the profits from your winning trades outweigh the losses from your losing trades. The most effective way to do this is to *cut your losses* and *let your profits run*, which is exactly what stop orders help you to do.

2

Stop Order to Sell

You can use stop orders both to buy into a position (next chapter) and to sell out of a position. I cover the sell case first, in this chapter, as this will be the most intuitive use of a stop order.

A **stop order to sell** is an order to sell a security when the price falls to a specified level. For long traders, the objective of using a **stop order to sell** is to stop a loss or secure a profit on an existing long position.

> For short traders, the objective is to establish a short position (sell short) when the price of a security is falling.

Who would use it, and why?

Many people think of a stop order as a stop loss order – they consider the stop order solely as a mechanism for getting out of a bad position. And that's the purpose of a *stop order to sell*: to limit your loss to a predetermined amount if the price falls rather than rises.

As the majority of successful traders will tell you, it is almost always better to cut your losses than it is to let them run. And whereas the prevailing wisdom is to "invest only what you can afford to lose", the use of a stop order allows you to invest more than you can afford to lose – providing that the stop gets you out of a bad position at a *loss* that you can afford to lose.

Stop orders to sell are used by short-term traders such as day traders, who want to get out very quickly if a trade turns against them. They may also be used by longer term investors as an if-all-else-fails safety net, just in case their fundamentals-driven value judgments prove to be wrong.

> For short traders, including spread bettors, a stop order to sell may be used to open a new short position rather than to close an existing long position.

Analogy – the Safety Net

Imagine that you're training to become a daredevil high wire act. While practicing on the rope strung 50 feet above the ground, you will be comforted by the presence of the safety net strung 20 feet below you at 30 feet above the ground.

You don't want to fall, of course. But if you do, you will suffer only hurt pride, and not broken bones or worse. In a nutshell, you'll live to try again.

A stop order to sell works exactly like this. The stop order (your safety net) is set at a distance below the share price (your tightrope) that you know is survivable; i.e. a fall to that level won't wipe you out.

What do you need to specify?

When you place a stop order with a broker you need to specify the *stop level*, which is the price (below the current market price) at which your position should be closed.

> For spread bettors and other long-and-short traders, the stop level would be the price at which an existing long position should be closed or at which a new short position should be opened.

When will it work?

Your use of a stop order to sell would be considered successful if:

- The price falls continuously (without gaps) so that your stop order triggers at or around the price you set, and then the price does not subsequently reverse.

- The price rises such that your stop order never actually triggers and you stay in profit.

Figure 4 shows the first successful case in which a stop order triggers as expected. Having observed the FTSE 100 index trading in notional range 5000 to 5500, we establish a long position at 5100 with a **stop order to sell** at 4900. When the index falls through the support level of 5000, our stop order triggers at 4900 limiting our loss to 200 points (or about 4%).

Figure 4: Stop Order to Sell, Success Scenario

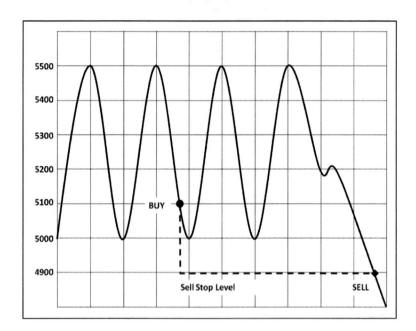

You should be able to visualise the second successful case, in which the stop order never actually triggers, without the aid of an illustration.

When might it not work?

Your use of a stop order to sell would be considered unsuccessful if:

*   The price falls suddenly (it 'gaps') so that your stop order triggers, but at a less favourable price than the price you set.

*   The price falls continuously (without gaps) so that your stop order triggers at or around the price you set; but the price subsequently recovers so that you need not have sold at all.

Guaranteed stops and stops-with-limits (Chapter 6) may be used alleviate the first of these problems, the gapping problem. The second problem has no automated solution, but you will find some tips on how to avoid the problem in Chapter 9.

Stop Order to Sell for Value Investors

The use of a stop order to sell is not restricted to technical traders who wish to sell when a stock breaks downwards out of a trading range. A stop order to sell might be placed by a value investor when he or she regards the stock in question to be overvalued, thereby using any price trend reversal – and the subsequent triggering of the stop order – merely as confirmation of their negative value judgement. Until such time as the true value is reflected by a falling price, the value investor can go on holding and banking the dividends having not sold out prematurely.

Not Limited to the FTSE 100 Index

Although this chapter and the subsequent chapters in this part of the book use the FTSE 100 Index for consistency across the theoretical examples, you should be aware that, in principle, stop orders can be used on any traded financial instrument. In any one of the examples I could easily have substituted a hypothetical price history for the Nikkei 225 index, or a specific stock like Bank of America, or price of gold, or the Euro/US Dollar foreign exchange currency pair.

As long as your broker allows stops orders on your chosen security, the order will operate as described in these examples. In Part 2 of this book you will find numerous examples of trading other markets including equities, commodities, currencies, and other indices.

Alternative Definition

At least one of the spread betting providers that I use defines a **stop order to sell** simply as:

An order that sells at a price less favourable than the current market price.

While strictly true, I believe that the negative connotations of this definition, however unintentional, do not do justice to the vital role of stop orders.

3

Stop Order to Buy

Having considered the *sell* case, I now consider the *buy* case with a **stop order to buy.**

As the mirror image of the **stop order to sell**, a **stop order to buy** is an order to buy a security when the price rises to a specified level. The objective of using a **stop order to buy** is to buy a security when its price is rising.

> For short traders the objective is to stop a loss or secure a profit on an existing short position. For the short trader, the 'stop order to buy' therefore performs the same function that the 'stop order to sell' performs for a long trader.

Who would use it, and why?

A trader who observes a stock, index or other security trading within a range would typically place a **stop order to buy** in order to effect an entry into a new (long) position when the price breaks out through the upper bound of the range. The theory is that a price is more likely to go on rising once it has broken through its upper resistance level.

When aiming to buy high / sell higher, a stop order to buy helps to fulfil the 'buy high' objective.

Analogy – What's Hot?

As a trader of financial instruments, or even of conventional goods like shoes, it pays to be aware of what is growing in popularity. When you see that something is starting to become fashionable there is money to be made in buying some of it today in order to sell it on for a higher price tomorrow, or next week, or next year.

The **stop order to buy** allows you to buy in to the anticipated future action when your chosen instrument is becoming 'in demand' as reflected by the rising price. When the price of shoes – or more realistically for this book, barrels of oil – rises above, say, $50, you want to know about it so that you can stock up in anticipation of further price rises.

What do you need to specify?

When you place a stop buy order with a broker you need to specify the *stop level*, which is the price (above the current market price) at which your position should be opened so that you will begin to benefit from any further rise.

> For spread bettors and other long-and-short traders, the stop level would be the price at which a new long position would be opened or at which an existing short position should be closed.

When will it work?

Your use of a **stop order to buy** would be considered successful if:

- The price breaks through its resistance point and continues rising rather than falling back.

- The stop order does not trigger because the price does not break out of its range.

Figure 5 shows the first successful case in which a stop order triggers as expected. Having observed the FTSE 100 index trading in the range 5000 to 5500, we place a stop order to buy at 5600. When the index breaks through the resistance level of 5500, our stop order triggers at 5600, thus establishing our long position in the uptrend.

Figure 5: Stop Order to Buy, Success Scenario

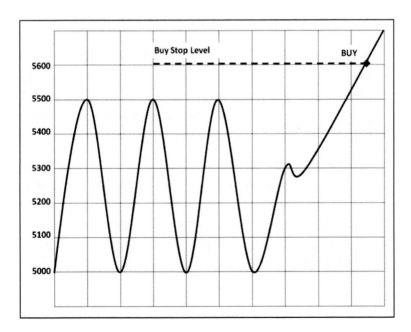

When might it not work?

Your use of a **stop order to buy** would be considered unsuccessful if:

- The price rises suddenly (it 'gaps') so that your stop order triggers, but at a less favourable price than the price you set.

- The price rises continuously (without gaps) so that your stop order triggers at or around the price you set; but the price subsequently falls back below the price at which your order executed.

Guaranteed stops and **stops-with-limits** may be used to alleviate the first of these problems, the gapping problem. The second problem has no automated solution, but you will find some tips on how to avoid the problem in Chapter 9.

Stop Order to Buy for Value Investors

The use of a **stop order to buy** is not restricted to technical traders who wish to buy when a stock breaks upwards out of a trading range. A value investor would be wise not to buy merely when a stock represents good value, but when the stock's price action confirms that the hidden value is starting to be recognised in the market.

So when all of the fundamentals stack up and your screening criteria are met, you might not buy the stock immediately. Place a **stop order to buy** that will trigger when the price rises by a defined amount, say 5%. You will not commit to the investment until the true value begins to be reflected in the rising stock price, and in the meantime you will not be disadvantaged if the price falls further thereby representing *even better value*.

Alternative Definition

As with the **stop order to sell** (previous chapter), at least one of the spread betting providers that I use defines a **stop order to buy** as simply:

An order that buys at a price less favourable than the current market price.

Again, I believe that the negative connotations of this definition do not do justice to the vital role of stop orders.

4

Trailing Stop Order to Sell

A **trailing stop order to sell** is an order to sell a security when the price falls by a specified amount.

The objective of a **trailing stop order to sell** is to track a rising price until it turns down, so as to sell at a high price at the onset of a new downtrend. For a long trader, a **trailing stop order to sell** would close an existing long position.

> For a short trader, this kind of order would open a new short position rather than close an existing long position.

Who would use it, and why?

A **trailing stop order to sell** would typically be used by a trend-following trader looking to secure an accrued profit at the point when the price of a security tops out and begins to fall. It addresses the problem that an unattended non-trailing **stop order to sell** would execute at a sub-optimal price if the price of the security rose significantly after the order was placed and then fell back to the original stop level.

When aiming to buy low / sell high, or buy high / sell higher, the **trailing stop order to sell** helps to fulfil the 'sell high' objective.

Analogy

Imagine again that you are an aspiring high wire acrobat. The higher the wire, the more you'll get paid for your show, so you're quite happy when your coach restrings the rope at 100 feet above the ground at your next practice session.

But wait a minute! The potential fall of 70 feet from the rope to the safety net originally strung at 30 feet could leave you permanently disabled. So naturally, you ask for the safety next to be raised up to 50 feet above the ground – or, once again, 20 feet below you. The most you could lose is 20 feet worth of pride.

A trailing stop order to sell works exactly like this. As the share price (your tightrope) rises higher, the stop order (your safety net) rises with it – automatically.

There is another analogy that I often use in relation to stop trailing stop orders; the analogy of a ratchet. A ratchet is a type of wrench that can freely turn in one direction but which stops (pun intended) turning when the direction is reversed. The trailing stop ratchet turns freely while the price rises, but stops – thereby selling you out – when the price starts to decline.

What do you need to specify?

When you give a trailing stop order to a broker you need to specify the *stop distance*, which is the distance below the (rising) market price at which your position should be closed.

> For spread bettors and other long-and-short traders, the stop distance would be the distance below the (rising) market price at which an existing long position should be closed or at which a new short position should be opened.

When will it work?

Your use of a **trailing stop order to sell** would be considered successful if:

- The price rises and never falls back by the trailing stop distance.

- The price rises and only falls back by the stop distance (thus triggering the sell order) when a genuine downtrend has established, and ideally – but not necessarily – when your position is in profit.

Figure 6 shows the first successful case. In this scenario we establish a long position in the FTSE 100 index at 5100, and place a **trailing stop order to sell** at a distance of 200 points below our buy-in price. As the price rises, the stop order is trailed upwards – either manually or automatically – so that it is never more than 200 points below the prevailing price. In this example the price never falls back quite far enough to trigger the stop order, and by the end of the chart we are assured a profit of almost 300 points above our original buy-in price.

Figure 6: Trailing Stop Order to Sell, Success Scenario

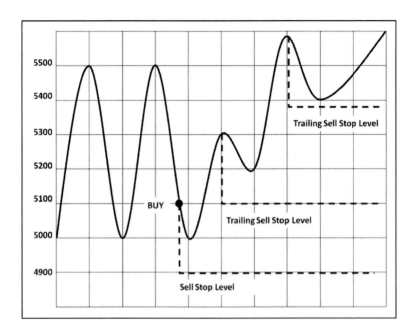

When might it not work?

Your use of a **trailing stop order to sell** would be considered unsuccessful if:

- The price falls suddenly (it 'gaps') so that your stop order triggers, but at a less favourable price than the price you set.

- The stop order triggers and then the price trend reverses, so that you need not have sold out at all.

Guaranteed stops and **stops-with-limits** may be used alleviate the first of these problems, the gapping problem. The second problem has no automated solution, but you will find some tips on how to avoid the problem in Chapter 9.

The Stop Gets Tighter as the Price Gets Higher

It is worth noting the mathematical fact that a **trailing stop order to sell** will get tighter in percentage terms as the price rises. A trailing stop set initially at 10 points below a price of 100 would sell on a 10% downturn; but by the time the price has doubled to 200 (lucky you), the same unaltered trailing stop would require only a 5% downturn in order to trigger.

Some traders will regard this as a good thing, because it allows less leeway in the fluctuating price as it gets more toppy. Some traders will want to adjust the stop distance so as to maintain a fixed percentage. You will find guidance on stop distances in Chapter 10.

5

Trailing Stop Order to Buy

As the mirror image of the **trailing stop order to sell,** a **trailing stop order to buy** is an order to buy a security when the prise rises by a specified amount.

For a long trader the objective of a **trailing stop order to buy** is to track a falling price until it turns up, so as to buy at a low price at the onset of a new uptrend.

> For a short trader, this kind of order would close an existing short position.

Who would use it, and why?

A trailing stop order to buy would typically be used by trend-following traders or bottom-fishing investors who are hoping to catch the point at which the price of a security bottoms out and begins to rise (e.g. the point at which a recovery stock begins to recover).

When aiming to buy low / sell high, the **trailing stop order to buy** helps to fulfil the 'buy low' objective.

What do you need to specify?

When giving a trailing stop buy order to a broker you need to specify the *stop distance*, which is the distance above the (falling) market price at which a new position should be opened.

> For spread bettors and other long-and-short traders, the stop distance would be the distance above the (falling) market price at which a new long position should be opened or at which an existing short position should be closed.

Analogy – What was NOT, is now HOT!

When considering the non-trailing **stop order to buy** in Chapter 3, I suggested that it allows you to buy something that has started rising in price – in order to benefit from any further price appreciation. When you place your **stop order to buy**, there is no guarantee that the price will rise to your specified level without falling first; and the more the price falls, the less attractive your original stop-buy level will become.

With the price of oil sitting at $45 a barrel, it might have made sense to place an order to buy automatically when the price rose to $50 a barrel. But if the price of oil fell to $35 a barrel before your original order executed, you would no doubt see an opportunity to revise your stop level down to $40 (i.e. to buy when the price rises to $40). Not only would you eventually buy at a much better price than that specified by your original stop order, but also (in this happy scenario) at a better price than if you had simply bought oil at the original market price of $45.

Revising down the target price of a **stop order to buy** in this way can be done by you manually, or it can be automated using your broker's **trailing stop order to buy**. Whether automated or not, a **trailing stop order to buy** allows you to track the price of an out-of-fashion instrument – a "what's not" instrument – until the positive price action indicates that it has once again become hot.

When will it work?

Your use of a **trailing stop order to buy** would be considered successful if:

- The price falls and only rises as far as the stop distance (thus triggering the buy order) when a genuine uptrend has established.

- The price falls all the way to zero without ever triggering the stop order.

Figure 7 shows the first successful case. We place a **stop order to buy** initially at 5600, just above the resistance level of the trading range. When the price falls to 4000 we revise the stop level downwards to 4200, and when the price falls further to 3500 we revise the stop level downwards again to 3700. If your broker allows *trailing* stop orders, these downward revisions would be effected automatically, as indicated by the greyed-out lines in this chart.

Figure 7: Trailing Stop Order to Buy, Success Scenario

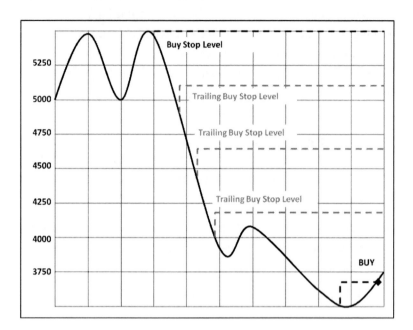

When might it not work?

You use of a **trailing stop order to buy** would be considered unsuccessful if:

- The price rises suddenly (it 'gaps') so that your stop order triggers, but at a less favourable price than the price you set.

- The stop order triggers and then the price trend reverses, so that you should not have bought in at all.

Guaranteed stops and **stops-with-limits** may be used to alleviate the first of these problems, the gapping problem. The second problem has no automated solution, but you will find some tips on how to avoid the problem in Chapter 9.

The Stop Gets Wider as the Price Gets Lower

It is worth noting the mathematical fact that a **trailing stop order to buy** will get wider in percentage terms as the price falls. A trailing stop set initially at 10 points above a price of 200 would buy on a 5% upturn; but by the time the price has halved to 100, the same unaltered trailing stop would require a larger 10% upturn in order to trigger.

As described in this chapter, a **trailing stop order to buy** would be used to buy a security when its price hits absolute rock bottom and then turns upwards. For some traders, a **trailing stop order to buy** may also be used to buy a security when its price falls significantly but temporarily before turning up again, i.e. to 'buy on the dips'.

6

Guaranteed Stop, and Stop with Limit

In the previous chapters I suggested that stop orders fail when markets gap. This is because stop orders are designed to guarantee *execution* but not *price*; which means that your stop order should definitely trigger when the threshold is crossed, but not necessarily at the price you intended. The order will execute at the *next available price*, which, if there has been a price gap or slippage in a fast moving market, may be quite different from the *last available price*.

In this chapter I'll introduce the idea of a price gap, and I'll explain how a **guaranteed stop** or a **stop-with-limit** might be used to alleviate the problem. You will find more practical advice on how to deal with price gaps in Chapter 9.

What is a Price Gap?

A price gap has occurred when the price of a security jumps apparently from one level to another (up or down) on little or no volume, without passing through the intermediate price points. Although gaps can occur at any time of day, most people's experience of price gaps will be when the day's opening price of a security does not match the previous day's closing price – as shown in Figure 8.

Having observed this market's low point at 5400 during Day 1, the trader sets a **stop order to sell** at 5350. Overnight the price gaps downwards to open the next day at 5100. Since the basic **stop order to sell** is not guaranteed, it executes at the opening price, 250 points below the intended stop level.

Figure 8: Overnight Price Gap

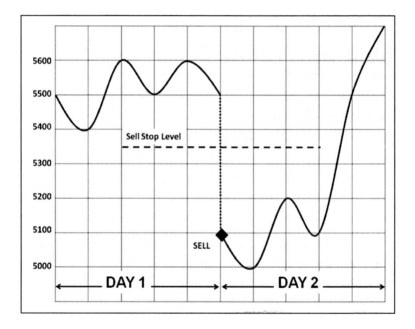

To add insult to injury in this scenario, the price recovers such that the trader need not have sold out at all, and now he holds no position from which he could benefit from the recovery.

Guaranteed Stop

A **guaranteed stop** is designed to guarantee execution *and price*. If your stop order triggers, it will execute at exactly the price you set – even if the market gaps.

In relation to the scenario described above, a guaranteed stop order would ensure that the trader's position would be closed at exactly 5350 as intended, thus saving him from an additional 250 point loss.

Your broker or spread betting provider is taking the risk here, so for this insurance against price gaps you will pay an additional premium – just as you would for any other insurance policy. The premium charge varies by broker and by market. For example, at the time of writing the charge levied by one spread betting firm is specified as *2 times quantity* on the UK 100 Rolling Spread, *0.30 times quantity* on the US SP 500 Rolling Spread, and *5 times quantity* on the GBP/USD (currency) Rolling Spread. It means that guaranteed stop on a £5-per-point spread bet would incur a premium of £10 on the UK 100 Rolling Spread, £1.50 on the US SP 500 Rolling Spread, or £25 on the GBP/USD Rolling Spread. You might also be obliged to set your **guaranteed stop order** initially at a specified minimum distance from the current market price.

Not all brokers allow guaranteed stop orders. Every broker is different. For example, they may allow a **guaranteed stop** on Prudential but not Aviva, on Persimmon but not Barratt, and on most if not all of the major indices and currencies.

Stop with Limit

This kind of order combines the features of a **stop order** with the features of a **limit order**; so that *if* the order triggers, then it executes within the limit you set or not at all. Contrast this with a **guaranteed stop order**, which will *definitely* execute, and at the exact price you set.

- A **stop order (with limit) to sell** is an order to sell a security when the price falls to a specified level (the stop level) providing the trade can be executed above a second lower level (the limit level).

- A **stop order (with limit) to buy** is an order to buy a security when the price rises to a specified level (the stop level) providing the trade can be executed below a second higher level (the limit level).

What do you need to specify?

For a **stop order (with limit) to sell** you specify the *stop level*, which is the price (below the current market price) at which your position should be closed. You also specify the *limit level*, which is the minimum price you are willing to accept for the sale.

For spread bettors and other long-and-short traders the *stop level* would be the price (below the current market price) at which a new short position should be opened or an existing long position closed. The *limit level* would be the minimum price at which you wish to open the short position or close the existing long position.

For a **stop order (with limit) to buy** you specify the *stop level*, which is the price (above the current market price) at which a long position should be opened. You also specify the *limit level*, which is the maximum price you are willing to pay to open the position.

> For spread bettors and other long-and-short traders the *stop level* would be the price (above the current market price) at which an existing short position should be closed or new long position opened. The *limit level* would be the maximum price at which you wish to close the existing short position or open a new long position.

Trailing Stop with Limits

Where your provider allows trailing stop orders you would specify a *stop distance* and a *limit distance* rather than a *stop level* and *limit level*.

It may be useful to look back at Figure 2 in Chapter 1, which shows a stockbroker order form for a **trailing stop with limit** order. Notice how the instructional text on the form is phrased as:

Sell when the share price falls a minimum of [stop distance].

Do not sell if the share price has fallen more than [limit distance].

When will it work?

Your use of a **stop-with-limit order** would be considered successful if:

- The market price gaps beyond your limit level, and therefore the stop order does not execute.

- The prices falls continuously towards your stop level and executes correctly at a price between your *stop level* and your *limit level*.

In Figure 9 I look again at the scenario presented in Figure 8. This time the trader sets a **stop order to sell** at 5350 with a limit at 5300. Overnight the price gaps downwards to open the next day at 5100. Since the price gap has breached the *limit level* as well as the *stop level*, the order does not execute; which is a good thing because the price subsequently recovers to close the gap.

Figure 9: Stop with Limit, Success Scenario

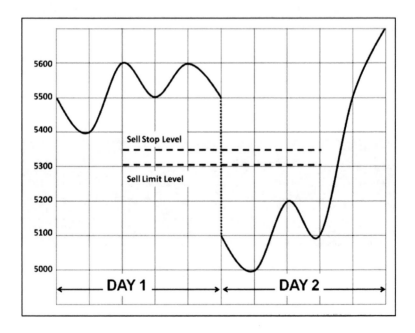

When might it not work?

This **stop-with-limit** order protects you from price gaps that subsequently close – as they often do. But these orders expose you to gaps that don't close.

Where a price goes on falling after a downward gap, you may have been better off selling out of a bad long position even at the unfavourable gapped-down price rather than holding on for further losses.

Guaranteed Stops and Price Slippage

Although I've described the benefits of **guaranteed stops** and **stops-with-limits** in terms of price gaps, I should note that **guaranteed stops** (but not **stops-with-limits**) also provide protection against price slippage – the fact that in fast-moving markets the price may have moved in-between the stop order being triggered and it actually being executed.

About 'Limit Profit' Orders

Many spread betting platforms allow you to attach two orders at the time you place a trade: a **stop-loss order** that will trigger if the price goes against you by a certain amount, and a **limit order** that will trigger if the price goes in your favour by a certain amount (thus crystallising your profit).

Because the input boxes from the *stop level* and *limit level* are usually presented side-by-side, it is easy to think that they are somehow connected – as in, this is a limit order that becomes effective if the stop is triggered, exactly as described in this chapter. But this is not the case. The limit order in this case is a plain old **limit order**, which is often termed a **limit profit order** because it is attached to a specific position.

7

Combining Stop Orders

The previous chapters described the various kinds of stop orders in isolation. In reality these orders would not necessarily be used in isolation, but more likely in combination, and possibly along with limit orders. In this chapter I present a selection of what I call *financial trading patterns*: combinations of orders that aim to solve a particular trading problem such as *buy low / sell high* or *buy high / sell higher*. These are patterns of trading activity; patterns of orders that you can apply in parallel or in sequence, rather than the chart patterns that you will see catalogued in other books.

The first pattern – Buy on Breakout / Sell if False – demonstrates how to use stop orders to solve that particular problem; the problem of 'how to buy on a breakout and then sell if the breakout proves to be false'.

Buy on Breakout / Sell if False

In this pattern the objective is to buy in to a rising price trend, signalled by a break through a resistance level, but to sell out at the earliest opportunity if the uptrend signal turns out to be false because the price falls back through the resistance level.

This scenario is shown in Figure 10. Having observed a trading range with a resistance level at 5400, we place a **stop order to buy** at 5500 so as to buy in to the rising trend when the price breaks out of the prior trading range. Once the position is established, we immediately place a **stop order to sell** at 5400 so as to close the position and cut our potential loss in the event that the breakout proves to be false.

In the figure, the solid line shows that the **stop order to sell** does execute in the event that the trend reverses. The dotted line shows that the **stop order to sell** does not execute in the event that the uptrend continues.

Figure 10: Buy on Breakout, Sell if False

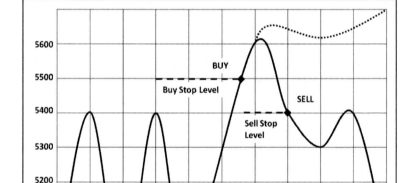

Buy Long or Sell Short

This one is for long-and-short traders, particularly spread bettors.

Where a price is oscillating within a tight trading range, a trader might conclude that the price will soon break out either upwards or downwards. As a long-and-short trader he might not actually care which way it goes, and he figures that he can profit either way. If the price breaks upwards through the resistance level he will establish a long position, and if the price break downwards through the support level he will establish a short position.

In Figure 11 the trader observes a tight trading range between 5200 and 5400, so he places a **stop order to buy** at 5500 and at the same time a **stop order to sell** at 5100. The solid line shows how a new long position is established if the price breaks through the resistance level and trends upwards. The dotted line shows how a new short position is established if the price falls through the support level and trends downwards.

Figure 11: Buy Long or Sell Short

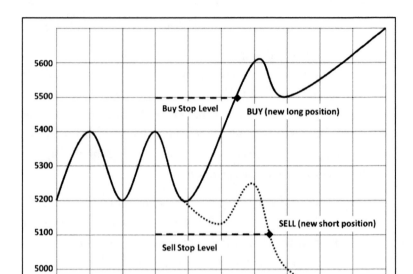

When applying this pattern beware that if the **stop order to buy** executes, the **stop order to sell** will still be left open and could trigger in the future; and vice versa. You might not see this as a problem, on the basis that the remaining sell order or buy order will automatically close your new position if the trend reverses – although in this case you would most likely want to adjust the stop level.

If you do see the vestigial order as a problem, your broker might allow you to do one of two things:

• Specify both orders as **good until** at the outset, for example *good for the day*; in which case either (or both) of the orders that don't execute will be deactivated automatically when the specified time has passed.

- Specify both orders at the outset together as a **one cancels other** (OCO) pair; in which case the successful execution of either order will cause the other order to be deactivated. An example OCO order form is given in Figure 12.

Figure 12: One Cancels Other (OCO) Order Form

Market: FTSE Rolling Daily (GBP) Rolling Spread **Current Price:** 5400 - 5401
New Order
Action: ⦿ Buy ⦾ Sell **Amount:** |1| **Level:** |5500|
☑ **OCO Order**
Action: ⦾ Buy ⦿ Sell **Amount:** |1| **Level:** |5100|

Buy Low / Sell High

In Chapter 5 I presented the **trailing stop order to buy** as a mechanism for *buying low*, and previously in Chapter 4 I presented the **trailing stop order to sell** as a mechanism for *selling high*. Here, I bring the two kinds of stop orders together in a trading pattern that aims to *buy low* and *sell high*.

The objective is to follow a falling trend down until it turns up, thereby hopefully *buying low*; and then to follow the rising trend until it turns down, thereby hopefully *selling high*.

This scenario is shown in Figure 13. Having deduced that a downtrend is underway, we set a stop order to buy at about 80 points (1.5%) above the current level of 5300. As the price trends down, we trail the stop level downwards, either manually (by adjusting our stop order to buy) or automatically (by placing an explicit **trailing stop order to buy**).

When the downtrend reverses, our stop order triggers and establishes a long position at about 5050, an improvement of 250 points (almost 5%) on the prevailing market price at the time we placed the order. We immediately place a **stop order to sell** at 80 points below our buy-in price.

As the price trends upwards, we trail the stop level upwards either manually or automatically. And when the uptrend reverses, our stop order triggers and closes out our position for a total profit of about 450 points.

In this scenario we have *bought low* and *sold high*.

> **!** As impressive as this may be, you should bear in mind that this is an idealised scenario. The numbers used are purely arbitrary, and have been chosen specifically to demonstrate a successful application of the pattern. Furthermore, the effect of the bid-ask spread and dealing charges have been omitted. Part 2 of this book considers the efficacy of patterns such as this one under *real market conditions*.

Figure 13: Buy Low / Sell High

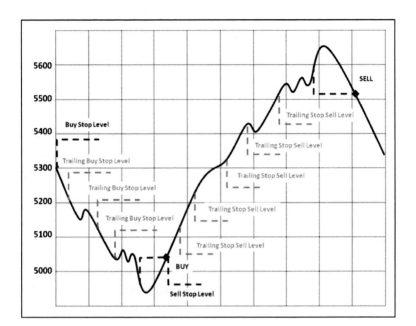

All Together Now

In the previous example I assumed that we held no position when we placed the initial **stop order to buy**. Now imagine that the prior price history had included a trading range, with our chart beginning just as the price fell through the prior support level.

As per the Buy Long / Sell Short pattern noted earlier, we might have established a net short position when the price broke downwards out of the trading range.

As per the Sell on Fall Through Support, Buy if False pattern (not given, but it's the inverse of the Buy on Breakout, Sell if False pattern noted earlier) we would have set a **stop order to buy** as insurance against the downtrend being false. *This could be the stop order to buy that you see at the beginning of the chart.*

In this new interpretation of the scenario, when the downtrend reverses and the **stop order to buy** executes, it closes the existing short position rather than opening a new long position.

But wait!

Suppose our existing short position was a $1-per-point spread bet, and we had set the **stop order to buy** for $2-per point. Execution of the order would close the existing short position and open a new long position for the balance of $1-per-point.

We profited on the downward leg, and now we stand to profit on the upward leg.

Now imagine that our **stop order to sell** which trails the rising price upwards is for $2-per-point. When the uptrend reverses, this order will close the current long position and open a new short position for the balance of $1-per-point. And so the cycle can begin again.

This combined pattern is logically sound, and it is perfectly possible to make money in this way. Possible, but not necessarily easy. It's a very difficult trick to pull off, which is why we will shortly move from *PART 1: Stop Orders and Theory* to *PART 2: Stop Orders in Practice*. In the next part I'll consider what we might *probably* achieve in practice rather than merely what we could *possibly* achieve in theory.

But first, a note about...

Multiple Exits

In the preceding examples I have described trading tactics that utilise stops in combination where one stop is used to enter a position (usually a **stop order to buy** for long traders) and the other stop is used to exit a position (usually a **stop order to sell**). But it is also possible to utilise two or more stops in combination, where they operate in the same direction – for example two **stop orders to sell**.

Suppose you devised a trading system in which you wished to exit a position if ever the price retraced by 10% from any peak, but in which you also wished to lose no more than 5% of your initial stake. You could implement this system with a **stop loss order to sell** at -5% *and* a **trailing stop order to sell** at -10%. The **stop loss order to sell** would limit your loss to 5% until the asset price had risen by 5.6%, at which point the **trailing stop order to sell** would take over and help you to run your profit.

In this scenario you just need to beware when one of the stop orders sells you out, that the other one is not left orphaned – thereby selling you back in (to a net short position) if its trigger price is ever breached.

Part Two

Stop Orders in Practice
(the Techniques)

8

Trading Timescales

The preface to this book stated that the book was aimed at three groups of market participants: traders, investors, and spread bettors. The applications of stop orders will be different depending on what kind of market participant you are, and in this chapter I explore how your use of stop orders will differ subtly over various timescales from short-term day-trading through intermediate-term swing trading to longer-term position trading and investing; and I also look at the unique characteristics of stop orders as they apply to spread bets.

Stop Orders for Traders

The umbrella term *trader* encompasses a range of trading styles and timescales from short-term day trading through to longer (potentially indefinite) position trading. In order to illustrate the use of stop orders in various trading scenarios I have classified the trading styles as day trading, swing trading, and position trading.

Some traders may argue about whether they agree with the classifications as I have described them. They might argue that a day trader can hold positions overnight, whereas I infer that he can't. They might argue that my swing trading examples in Chapter 12 and Chapter 13 are over too long or too short a timescale, or that swing trading can be effective in a trending market even though I imply that it can't. They might argue that my description of position trading should actually be labelled as trend-following.

These kinds of arguments don't really matter.

What is important is that – however we choose to label them – there are different trading styles that operate over different periods of time, and that stop orders will be utilised somewhat differently according to the trading style.

Day Traders

Hardcore day traders aim to trade several times per day – and maybe even several times per hour – before closing all of their open positions at the end of the trading day. These traders try to judge whether a price will go up or down in the very near future and will typically place very tight stop orders so as to exit bad positions at the earliest possible opportunity. Since tight stops are prone to being triggered unfavourably due to price gaps (see next chapter) it is important not to leave positions and orders open overnight. Where day traders use stop orders, these are likely to be placed as **Good For the Day** (GFD) or even to expire at a particular time within the current day.

Non-professional day traders are likely to be spread bettors, who do not incur dealing charges, who do not have to account for tax on profitable trades, and who can place orders that expire at an exact time of day. They are also likely to trade short (bet on falling prices) as well as long (bet on rising prices). The fact that trades get stopped out frequently need not worry day traders, because they monitor the markets continually throughout the day looking for opportunities to establish new positions.

Swing Traders

Swing traders are looking for medium-term price swings in non-trending markets. They will place wider stops than day traders, most likely corresponding with observed support and resistance levels; and they will use **stop orders** in conjunction with **limit orders**. Swing trading may be implemented using spread betting, or for a large trading range it may be feasible to use a regular equity trading account (bearing in mind the additional dealing charges).

The long swing trader's strategy might be as follows:

1.   Place a **limit order to buy** just above the support level, to buy-in towards the bottom of the trading range.

2.   Place a **stop order to sell** just below the same support level, to close the long position if the price does not rebound from the support level as anticipated but instead falls through the support level to establish a new downtrend.

3.   Place a **limit order to sell** just below the resistance level, to close the long position at a profit.

A short swing trader would place a **limit order to sell** just below the resistance level, with a **stop order to buy** just above the resistance level (to close a bad short position) and a **limit order to buy** just above the support level (to close the short position at a profit).

In Figure 14 you can see the swing trading pattern applied to the FTSE 100 index over the period May to June 2009. Having seen the index peak at 4520, then trough at 4300, and then peak again at 4510, the trader sets a **limit order to buy** at 4340 and a **limit order to sell** at 4480 so as to hopefully capture a 140-point profit in the next up-cycle. By way of protection he places a **stop order to sell** at 4280, so as to close out his long position if the price continues to fall after the buy order executes.

As a long-and-short trader, his initial **limit order to buy** takes the form of a £1-per-point spread bet and his initial **limit order to sell** is a £2-per-point spread bet – so that sell order not only closes his long position but also establishes a new short position for the balance of £1-per-point, thereby allowing him to capture another 140 points of profit in the downward leg. This short trade would be closed by a subsequent **limit order to buy** of £2-per-point placed again at 4340 in order to establish a new net long position of £1-per-point at the bottom of the cycle.

This alternating long-and-short cycle can repeat until the price breaks out of the trading range either upwards or downwards; which is where the **stop order to sell** (placed just below the trading range) and it's complementary **stop order to buy** (placed just above the trading range) come in handy. On 16 June the **limit order to buy** at 4340 establishes a new long position, but the price continues to fall – below the established trading range – and the **stop order to sell** automatically closes his position at 4280 thus taking him out of the market until he can determine what the new price pattern is.

Figure 14: Swing Trading Pattern, with Stop on Breakout – FTSE 100 Index

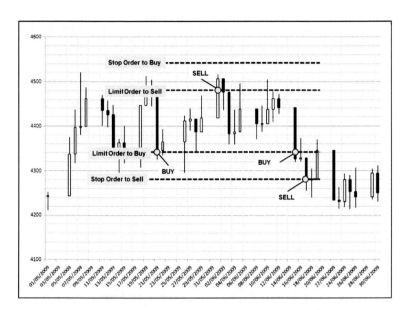

This series of trades has netted the trader a profit of 140 points (up-cycle) plus 140 point (down-cycle) minus 60 points (the difference between the final **limit order to buy** and **stop order to sell**). End result: a profit of 200 points, or £200 (ignoring the bid-ask spread). Obviously he could have scaled up the profit for the month to £2000 by placing £10-per-point and balancing £20-per-point spread bets rather than £1-per-point and £2-per-point spread bets.

I've described this swing trading pattern in spread betting terms, because this is perhaps the most cost-effective way to implement the pattern. If you do not have access to a spread betting account, you'll have to talk to your brokers about whether they will allow you to establish short positions. Even if they don't, there may be a solution in the form of exchange traded funds as follows.

Swing Trading with ETFs

Exchange Traded Funds allow traders and investors to establish a position in a pool of securities such as the stocks comprising a major index, just like conventional mutual funds do. Unlike conventional mutual funds, ETFs can be traded throughout the day just like equities via a regular stockbroker account.

Some providers of exchange traded funds offer inverse-tracking funds that effectively let you establish short positions in major indices. Examples include:

- DB X-TRACKERS FTSE 100 SHORT ETF (ISIN code LU0328473581)

- DB X-TRACKERS SHORTDAX ETF (ISIN code LU0292106241)

which you should be able to trade via your regular broker by entering the relevant codes.

If you intend to apply the swing trading pattern described above using short ETFs, take note that you would be establishing short positions by *selling* 1 x the *DB X-TRACKERS FTSE 100 ETF* and *buying* 1 x the *DB X-TRACKERS FTSE 100 SHORT ETF* rather than by selling 2 x the *DB X-TRACKERS FTSE 100 ETF.*

From Swing Trading to Position Trading

In the swing trading pattern just described, when the price breaks upwards from the resistance level or downwards through the support level, a net long or short position is established in order to benefit from the anticipated uptrend or downtrend.

This can no longer be described as swing trading, and is better described as position trading in which the aim is to ride the trend for as long as possible.

Position Traders

I would describe myself primarily as a position trader who has no fixed timescale for closing a trade. I'll ride the uptrend as far as it goes, and then (maybe) ride the downtrend with a short position. You might think that this does not sound that different from the swing trading described above, but it's different in the following respects:

- The *swing trader* has observed a trading range and uses **limit orders** to buy or sell at the limits of the range.

- The *position trader* believes that 'the trend is your friend', but has no idea how long the current trend (up or down) will last. The objective is to join the trend using a stop order, to maintain the position by trailing the stop order manually or automatically, and to exit the position using a stop order when the trend reverses.

The position trader might be a spread bettor, a conventional equity investor, or an index investor who trades exchange traded funds. The important thing, for this book, is that the trading vehicle allows stop orders, which rules out conventional mutual funds and covered warrants (a form of *option*). That said, even for financial instruments that do not permit stop orders, the idea of a stop-out or stop-in level can be useful. [See the Mental / Maunal Stops section later in this chapter.]

Since a position trader has no specific timescale for opening or closing a position, he is likely to place stop orders as **Good Till Cancelled** (GTC) or for the maximum period allowed by the broker – for example, valid for 30 days. In the latter case, the position trader would need to replace his expired stop orders on a monthly basis so as not to lose the protection they provide.

As a position trader, I would typically employ a tight stop initially (to guard against being wrong) and then widen the stop – while at the same time raising it – as the profit accumulates.

Stop Orders for Investors

Investors are likely to establish long positions based on criteria other than price action; for example, based on company fundamentals. They are unlikely to establish short positions and are likely to invest using a regular stock trading account or a mutual funds supermarket.

The decade from 1999 to 2009 showed that investing on a Long Term Buy and Hold (LTBH) basis is fraught with danger. An investment in the Dow Jones or FTSE index in 1999 would have been down some 40% as of March 2009, and an investment made two years earlier in 1997 would only just be breaking even after 12 years. Admittedly these investors would have banked some dividends along the way, but imagine that their buy-and-hold investments had been in the banks and other financial institutions that suffered massively during the 2007-2008 financial crisis. No amount of dividends would make up for the 90% to100% capital depreciation in some cases.

The moral of the story is that even long-term investors should have some regard for the prevailing trend, and would be wise to employ wide stop orders if only as an if-all-else-fails safety net.

This may have been particularly important to you when you took that extended two-month vacation in Mexico during May and June 2008, and returned to find that your portfolio of financial stocks – which you had bought a few months earlier when they offered something like 35% 'better value' than at their peaks – had fallen by another 50% while you were away. A protective stop order at 20% below the prevailing price could have saved you a lot of money. And on some stocks saved you from a total wipeout, during the period when you had no opportunity to rebalance your portfolio in the light of unfolding events.

Stop Orders for Growth Investors

We have established that stop orders may be useful to investors as an if-all-else-fails safety net to guard against a previously sound stock or other security that falls on hard times. It's what we might regard as an end-of-life stop order.

A tighter stop order may be applicable at the time that an investment is first made. Michael Moe, author of *Finding the Next Starbucks*, is a growth investor who nonetheless advises that "cutting losses early on mistakes is critical to avoiding the crushing effects of negative returns". This idea of taking small losses quickly on bad positions is second nature to traders, but it may not be what you generally expect to hear from an 'investor'.

Investors and the Moral High Ground

I recently read an article[1] on the UK's Motley Fool website (**www.fool.co.uk**) titled "Investing is not Gambling". The implication is that true *investors* take *honest profits* year after year from companies that they own for the long term through thick and thin thereby supporting the economy, whereas traders are merely speculators, or even worse – immoral gamblers.

Well, in 2007 it turned out that investors' 'honest' profits (collected as dividends) from banks and other financial institutions turned out to be not so honest after all. And while it might have been morally satisfying to continue holding on to the bastion of the British high street known as Woolworths, it would have been a total disaster from a financial point of view when the shares fell to zero!

There is nothing immoral about using stop orders to protect your own financial position.

---

[1]http://www.fool.co.uk/news/investing/investing-strategy/2009/05/13/investing-is-not-gambling.aspx

Stop Orders for Spread Bettors

Stop orders are of vital importance to spread bettors as a mechanism for limiting losses. As a leveraged product, placing a spread bet does not require you to have funds available to cover the whole of your potential loss on a trade. A spread bet gone wrong can quickly bankrupt you if you really don't have sufficient funds available to meet the provider's margin call.

As a concrete example, imagine that you placed a long bet for $1-per-point bet on Freddie Mac at 6000 in 2007. Your maximum potential loss in case of a total wipe-out (not as fanciful as it once seemed) would be $6000. Yet the spread betting provider does not require you to have the full $6000 on account with them in order to place the bet. They require you to have funds to cover a *margin* of say 25%, therefore only $1500. Since you only have to deposit 25% of the required amount, this bet is effectively leveraged at '4 times'. Which means that your profits – and losses! – would accrue four times as fast as a conventional investment.

Due to the risk of accumulating runaway losses, spread betting providers will typically place a **stop-loss order** automatically on any positions that you open; and in 'limited risk' spread betting accounts this is likely to be a **guaranteed stop loss order.** The automatic placement of this stop-loss order will typically be based on 80% (to allow for slippage) of your available funds, or 80% of a market-specific and broker-specific Maximum Computer Generated Stop-Loss (Max CGSL). These automatic stop-loss orders are effectively good-till-cancelled and cannot be removed, but you can usually adjust them (in either direction) to your own desired level.

Note that I just used the term **stop loss order** rather than merely **stop order.** Some spread betting providers define a **stop loss order** as being a **stop order** that is attached to a particular position (i.e. a stop order that is placed at the time the position is opened). This is an important distinction because a **stop loss order** would be cancelled if the associated position is closed manually, whereas a standalone stop order applied to the same security – but not placed at the time a position was established – would remain in force till its 'good until' time had passed.

A spread bettor may well trade short as well as long, and might trade currencies and commodities in addition to equities and stock indices. But spread betting is a trading vehicle, rather than a trading style such as day trading, swing trading or position trading. All trading styles – including, I would argue, investing – are possible with a spread betting account.

Unless I say otherwise, whenever I mention spread bets in this part of the book I am referring to *rolling* spread bets that stay open indefinitely until you close them. Holding positions on these spread bets is rather like holding stakes in the underlying equities themselves; your bet does not have to come good within a specific timeframe, and nor is your profit limited by having to close the position prematurely. Long spread bettors pay a small daily interest charge to hold rolling spread bets, but I regard this as negligible compared with the leveraged profits that are possible, and for equities and indices it can be offset by the dividends that are received on long positions. The daily interest charge would become problematic in the case where a position stays around the same price level for an extended period of time, i.e. in the case that the price neither rises (in which case the leveraged capital appreciation would outweigh the interest charges) nor falls (in which case the position would be closed by the stop order). In this situation a time-based stop-out policy may be beneficial, as described shortly.

Short spread bettors receive a daily interest charge in relation to their rolling spread bets, and they pay dividends when due on equity and index spread bets.

Life Cycle of a Trade – from Entry to Exit

All traders and investors think about trade entry: what to buy and when to buy it. While stop orders cannot help you to decide *what to buy*, they certainly allow you to specify *when to buy it*.

Some traders and investors – but not enough – also think about trade exit: when to sell-up and move on. A stop order allows you to specify in advance the price at which you would like to sell-up and move on.

> Don't forget that a short trader would enter a trade by deciding 'what to sell and when to sell it' and would subsequently exit by deciding 'when to buy-up and move on'.

It's not all about entries and exits, and many traders fail to consider what happens between trade entry and trade exit. They give scant attention to *trade maintenance*.

Aside from their use as mechanisms for entry and exit, stop orders may also be used just as effectively to maintain a trade; for example to secure an increasing amount of profit as a trade progresses without actually having to crystallise the profit by closing the position prematurely.

The consideration that you give to the full life cycle of a trade – from entry, through maintenance, to exit – will depend on your trading style. For a day trader, it may be predominantly about the entries and exits, whereas for a long-term investor those entries and exits may be few and far between, with every position being effectively in long-term maintenance.

Trade Maintenance: Pyramiding

In a leveraged (e.g. spread betting) portfolio, the application of stop orders on existing positions may also free up additional funds for re-investment in the same or other positions during the maintenance phase. Greater gains may be achieved by pyramiding in this way.

You will find a real-life pyramiding example in Chapter 12. In the meantime I will tell you that the basic technique is as follows:

- You invest £1000 in ABC plc at a price of 100 with no stop order, so your value at risk is the full £1000.

- When the price rises to 150, you place a break-even stop at 100, thus reducing your value at risk to zero.

- Notionally, at least, you have freed up another £1000 worth of risk capital, so you can make a new, additional £1000 investment for no more than your original risk.

The upshot is that you now have £2000 working for you, but you are risking only £1000 of it.

I consider my own position trading strategy to be working when I spend more time in the maintenance phase – adjusting my stop orders and adding to my existing positions – than I spend executing my entries and exits. Adjusting my stop orders so as to protect existing positions costs me nothing in terms of transaction costs and the bid-ask spread, yet with every turn of the screw I feel that I am in a real sense *making money*.

> Don't underestimate the power of the stop order as a cure for over-trading. When you get itchy fingers and feel that you simply have to do something in the market, think about relieving your itch by tweaking your protective stops rather than placing a new trade. It works for me.

Trade Maintenance: Part–Closing

Another trade maintenance technique that has implications for stop orders is 'part-closing'. In a sense, this technique is the opposite of pyramiding since it involves reducing the size of your position as the price rises.

The idea here is to lock-in some profit by closing part of a profitable position, or – in the context of stop orders – to lower our break-even point thus allowing for a wider stop that is less likely to get triggered. It works like this:

Suppose you place a £2-per-point long spread bet on gold at a price of 1000, with a **stop-loss order** at 980. The gold price rises to 1020 and you sell half of your position for a profit of 20 points. You can now choose between:

- Raising your stop to your original purchase price of 1000, thereby allowing you to keep the crystallised 20 points even if your remaining half-position falls to break-even.

- Leaving your stop at 980, thereby having a wider 40-point stop that is less likely to get triggered but which will still allow you to break-even overall.

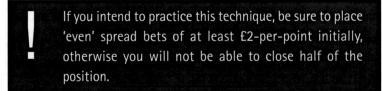

If you intend to practice this technique, be sure to place 'even' spread bets of at least £2-per-point initially, otherwise you will not be able to close half of the position.

This technique need not be limited to spread betting accounts, and you could practice the part-closing technique in a regular brokerage account – by specifying a number of shares (or value of shares) to sell rather than choosing the Sell All option.

If you exit manually, don't forget to cancel your stop(s)!

In a pure stop-based trading strategy, the only time you will exit a position is when your stop order triggers. But of course there are circumstances in which you will exit a position (close a trade) manually before your closing stop order is triggered. You might consider a position to be significantly over-valued (for a long trade) or under-valued (for a short trade) on fundamental grounds, and so you might decide to take your profit. Or you might simply need the money for other, better, opportunities, or even to pay the rent.

One of the most common errors made in relation to stop orders is to not cancel an outstanding stop order on a trade that you close manually. For a long-only trader or investor operating via a regular brokerage account this might not be a problem because it is not possible to establish a net short position. But in a long-and-short trading account, such as a spread betting account, this can be a real problem. If you close your £1-per-point long spread bet manually and leave a £1-per-point stop order in place, your stop order could trigger in due course, thus establishing a new unintentional short position for £1-per-point. And it can happen the other way too. If you close your £1-per-point short spread bet manually and leave a £1-per-point stop order in place, your stop order could trigger in due course thus establishing a new, unintentional long position for £1-per-point.

As mentioned earlier, it is for this reason that most, if not all, spread betting providers will distinguish between a **stop loss order** (which is attached to a specific trade, usually when the trade is opened) and a **stop order** (which is entirely standalone). The former **stop loss order** will be cancelled automatically when the associated open trade is closed; however the trade is closed. The latter **stop order** will remain in force *until you cancel it*.

You might wonder, therefore, why it is not compulsory to attach every stop order to an open trade as a **stop loss order**. But if you look back at the swing trading example earlier in this chapter, you will see that there are some trading strategies in which you might want a degree of asymmetry between opening and closing trades, i.e. you want a stop order to close an existing long position and establish a net short position. Or vice versa.

The lesson: be very careful to always monitor what stop orders you have pending.

Which Financial Instruments Allow Stop Orders?

In theory, a broker could provide stop orders on any tradable financial instrument, whether an underlying security or a derivative instrument. In practice you'll find that they don't. Or that they provide stop orders but not trailing stop orders. I seem to remember once having to fill out a specific disclaimer form before my broker would enable this *advanced* feature. Even within a specific security type, such as equities, you might find that your broker allows stop orders on some equities but not others.

This is obviously an important consideration when choosing your investment vehicles. There is little point devising a stop-based trading or investment strategy using mutual funds or leveraged covered warrants if you then find that your broker does not allow stop orders on them.

I cannot speak for every broker, and in any case the list may change over time, but at the time of writing I can tell you that my UK broker allows **stop orders** and **trailing stop orders** on *individual equities* and *exchange traded funds except where they are dollar denominated*, but not on *mutual funds, covered warrants* (a form of options), *exchange traded commodities* or *investment notes* (which are structured products).

When it comes to spread betting, you will find that most, if not all, spread betting providers allow stop orders on most, if not all, markets – which includes equities, indexes, currencies, and commodities. But not all of them provide trailing stop orders.

Just because your broker does not allow automated stop orders on certain financial instruments, or your spread betting provider does not allow automated trailing stops, does not mean that you can't use the *idea* of stops and trailing stops as part of your investment strategy.

Mental / Manual Stops

Setting stop-out points allows you to take a disciplined approach to defining your exit strategy at the time you enter a trade. Remember that if you "fail to plan your exit, you plan to exit in failure". Where your broker does not provide automated stop orders, you might decide to make a mental (or written) note of your intended stop levels and then apply those orders manually by placing *market orders* at the right time.

As you enter each position, you might set a mental stop and possibly write it down in your *stop orders notebook*. Each day, or week, or month, depending on your trading horizon, you would compare the current prices of your positions against the stop-out points that you had noted. If a position has crossed its stop-out point, you would close the position. This is exactly what your broker does when you place an automated stop order, except that it is all done electronically on a minute-by-minute basis.

By managing your mental stops manually in this way, you open up the possibility of incorporating any financial instrument into your stop-based strategy. The techniques described in this book could be applied to the mutual funds in your funds supermarket account. You lose something in fidelity and accuracy, because the price might move far beyond your stop-point before you have had chance to check it, or in this case because the fund price might move in the 24 hours after you instruct the fund manager to sell. But you gain the assurance that your stop orders will never be executed automatically at unfavourable prices due to price gaps (next chapter).

Managing your own stop order book can obviously be very labour-intensive, but there is commercial software that will allow you to enter your desired stop levels and will *signal* you when a position should be closed. Some online brokers also allow you to set stock alerts so that you receive an email when your specified price level is breached, but no trade is executed automatically.

Obviously a manually managed stop order book is of no use to a day trader; but the idea of a mental stop might be. When trading a single security, a day trader might decide to stop out when the price falls by (for example) 20 points, and will hover his mouse cursor over the *sell* button in case it does.

The prior discussion is phrased in terms of 'stopping out of' long trades. But the idea of managing stop orders manually can also apply to 'stopping in to' long trades and 'stopping in to' or 'stopping out of' short trades.

Continuing the long-trading scenario: As your positions move in to profit, you might revise your manually noted stop-out points upwards (and never downwards for long trades) so as to break even or to secure some profit. In effect you are manually implementing your own **trailing stop orders.**

If your broker allows stop orders but not trailing stop orders, you would place automated stop orders with them but you would trail these orders manually by adjusting the stop levels of those orders as and when necessary.

Trailing your stop orders manually has an added advantage: it gives you something to do in the market. If you are an impatient trader, you could make the adjustment of your stop levels part of your daily routine. Not only will it soothe your itchy fingers without incurring dealing charges, but it may also give you the buzz that, with each adjustment, you are notionally making money – in the sense that the higher your stop level (for a long position) the more profit you have secured. This kind of therapy does work for me and my itchy fingers, and it might work for you too. Just don't become too obsessive about adjusting your stop orders to levels that are not justified by the chart support levels or whatever other criteria you use.

> There is another advantage to spending more timing maintaining your existing positions (by adjusting your stops) rather than entering and exiting new positions: the fact that you are not at the mercy of the broker's reliability. If your trading style requires you to enter and exit trades rapidly, you may well find that the broker's website ceases to function – or they stop answering the telephones – just when you most need to open or close a position urgently.

One final point about mental stops: In his book *The Way to Trade*, John Piper advises that inexperienced traders should not rely on mental stops and should place stops "in the market" at the time they place their trades. This is sound advice if your broker allows you to place stop orders, because novice traders (and even some professionals) are notoriously bad at actually pulling the trigger when their mental stop levels are breached.

Other stop ideas

While on the subject of mental stops, it is worth mentioning that some traders have conceived alternative stop types that are generally not provided by brokers as automated stops – therefore they must be implemented as mental stops. Two of these alternative stop ideas are:

Time Stops – such as those used by day traders. You will exit a position at the end of the trading day, or, for example, after one week has elapsed and your profit-target stop has not already been triggered.

Moving Average Stops – that would buy you in to (for long traders) or out of (for short traders) a position when, for example, the 20-day moving average price crosses upwards through the 200-day moving average price; or which would sell you out of (for long traders) or in to (for short traders) a position when the 20-day moving average price crosses downwards through the 200-day moving average price.

Note that while these kinds of stop orders are provided by few, if any, brokers, it may be possible to implement them using a trading software package such as TradeStation (**www.tradestation.com**). The program would signal you to enter or exit a position when your stop-out condition is met.

Coincidentally, I recently received an email from one of my spread betting providers reminding me of their website's *technical analysis* feature – it will alert you when certain patterns appear in the price charts you are following. This might just offer a way to 'stop-in' manually on the appearance of a 'double-bottom' formation, for example.

What Kind of Trader are You?

My implicit advice is that the road to success is to *not* artificially set a trading timescale in advance, but rather to cut losses and let profits run as a position trader. That's what works for me, but it might not work for you.

Everyone is different. Some people have ample time each day to trade or to analyse stocks, and some people don't. Some people like the cut-and-thrust of ultra-short-term day trading, and some people don't. Some people couldn't care less about the ongoing machinations of the stock markets, and they simply want their 'investments' to be *safe*.

The key is to understand what style of trading suits you, and to use stop orders in a way that is appropriate for your chosen trading style.

Key Points

- Stop orders are applicable to all trading styles and time horizons.

- Stop orders are not offered by all brokers on all financial instruments.

- Mental / manual stops are useful where automated stop orders are not available.

- It is possible to conceive other kinds of stops that are not provided by brokers but which can be implemented mentally or using trading software.

9

Price Gaps and Whipsaw Losses

When documenting the types of stop orders in Chapters 2 through 5 I pointed out that those orders could prove ineffective in the face of price gaps. And then in Chapter 6 I presented **guaranteed stop orders** and **stop-with-limit orders** as possible solutions, subject to these being offered by your broker.

In this chapter I look again at price gaps, and an associated issue of whipsaw losses, from a more practical perspective. This discussion of price gaps and whipsaw losses, and specifically the avoidance of both, will lead us into deeper discussion of placing stop orders at appropriate levels in the next chapter. But before we can discuss the stop placement solution(s), we must define the problem by asking...

What is a Price Gap, and When Does it Occur?

A gap occurs when a price jumps (up or down) from one level to another without apparently passing through the intermediate price points; the implication for stop orders being that, when a gap occurs, the order has no chance to execute at the price you set. Since a stop order guarantees *execution* but not *price*, the order *will execute* but at an *unfavourable price*. To make matters worse, the gap may turn out to be a *spike*; in which case the price shoots up or down, triggers your order at an unfavourable level, and then returns almost immediately to the previous level.

Price gaps can occur at different times for different reasons. Here are two possible reasons:

1. A trader or investor operating a regular stock trading account might witness an overnight price gap – where the next day's opening price is notably different from the previous night's closing price. Although a spread bettor may see no gap on his chart at all (because the spread betting chart may include out-of-hours trading prices).

2. Unexpected bad (or good) news during market hours, or just before the market opens, might rattle the market makers and leave them temporarily unable to determine an accurate price; in which case they may widen the bid-ask spread causing the offer price to simultaneously gap up (the price you would pay to buy) and the bid price to gap down (the price you would receive if you sold).

> **!** Note that the likelihood that you will be affected by price gaps will depend on what you are trading. Foreign exchange markets that have very high liquidity and 24-hour trading will be less susceptible to gapping than lightly traded stocks.

Stop order adjustments following corporate actions such as bonus issues

Another interesting time that a chart will show a price gap is when a share price has become diluted due to a rights issue, or the price of the shares has been halved or doubled (or any other multiple) for purely technical reasons as a result of a share split or consolidation. Since the gap in these cases is entirely expected, is purely technical in nature, and has no effect on the value of your holdings, it raises the question of whether your broker or spread betting provider will trigger your stop order under such conditions, or whether they will automatically adjust the stop level to bring it in to line with the new adjusted price level. In other words, when a share price splits from $2 to $1 with the value of your holding totally unaffected (because you are granted twice as many new shares), will your stop order at $1.90 be triggered, thus closing your position, or will it be adjusted to a level of $0.90 (the same 10 cents difference) or $0.95 (the same 5% difference)? I can't answer this question for you, but your broker should be able to.

In a similar vein, you will find that equity positions will gap down for purely technical reasons when the stock in question goes ex dividend, to reflect the fact that future purchasers of the stock will not be entitled to the dividend.

A Tale of Three Traders

The best way to show how price gaps can affect traders is through a series of realistic scenarios. I've not forgotten about investors here, who may have something in common with the ETF Trader in the first example.

The ETF Trader

He (or she, I'm not being sexist!) trades major indices using exchange traded funds (ETFs) via a regular brokerage account. He watches the FTSE 100 index during the day on 17 August 2009, and just after the market closes he sets a **stop order to buy** not far above what he considered to be the most recent resistance level of 4640; so as to buy-in if the price breaks upwards out of the trading range.

The chart in Figure 15 shows that overnight the price gaps upwards by 40 points, thus triggering his **stop order to buy** the next morning with potentially a 40 point price disadvantage compared with the level he set. As he examines the unveiling chart, he is disconcerted to see that the price now appears to have started falling (to close the gap). He concludes that perhaps his stop order triggered unnecessarily at the unfavourable price.

> Note that in this example I use a price chart of the FTSE 100 index itself, which shows the price gap quite clearly, and which corresponds with the spread bettor's chart that you will see shortly. In reality, an ETF trader would trade an ETF (such as the iShares FTSE 100 ETF or DB X-TRACKERS FTSE 100 ETF) as a proxy for the underlying index. He would therefore set his stop orders according to the prices on the charts for those instruments.

Figure 15: Overnight Price Gap – FTSE 100 Index

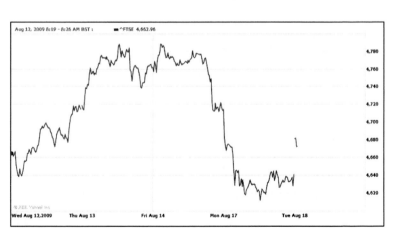

Source: Yahoo! Finance UK & Ireland

So what can the trader do to avoid this situation?

Well, to start with, he might not need to do anything. Some brokers hold fire on automatic stop orders during the first minutes of trading each day until prices settle down. But the trader might not want to rely on this assumption.

As mentioned previously, he could have placed a **guaranteed stop order** if this was allowed by the broker; otherwise a **stop-with-limit order** if this was allowed. But he should remember that the latter will offer protection against gaps that close but not against those that don't. If the scenario played out differently (and in this case it subsequently did) so that the gap did not close he may well find that buying in at the unfavourable gapped-up price would have been preferable to not buying into a continuing uptrend at all.

In the absence of **guaranteed stops** and **stops-with-limits** the ETF trader is surely at the mercy of overnight gapping. He must simply accept that he may get stopped into (or out of) a position at an unfavourable price, and maybe for no good reason if the gap closes. But he does have another option: remove or adjust the stop order before the market opens if he thinks that the opening price will be substantially different from the previous day's closing price.

Figure 16, which is a spread bettor's chart of the same two-day time period, shows that the FTSE 100 index price actually followed a winding but more continuous path upwards during the extended trading hours after 4.30pm on 17 August and before 8.00am on 18 August.

Spread bettors in the UK can trade the FTSE 100 index and other major international indices for additional hours after the markets close at 4.30pm.

Figure 16: Spread Bettor's Chart of the Overnight Price Gap – FTSE 100 Index

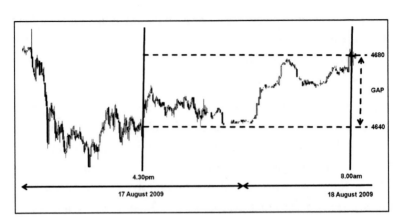

So from the spread bettor's point of view there was no gap at all. Or, to put it another way, access to the spread trader's out-of-hours chart would allow the ETF trader to anticipate the opening gap, and – just before the market opens – remove or relax the stop order that would now surely trigger at an unfavourable price. An ETF trader might benefit from opening a spread trading account, if only to gain an insight into the overnight price action.

In a similar vein, a stock trader might consider removing or relaxing a stop order on an equity that is about to issue a trading statement or annual results before the market opens. If the price gaps up or down on good or bad news, the stop order may well have executed at an unfavourable price. The trader should, of course, reinstate the stop order as soon as the news has been priced in to the market.

Unfortunately, without the benefit of a crystal ball it not possible to anticipate unexpected news about a particular stock. A good illustration of this occurred on 7 September 2009 when Cadbury shares gapped up by more than 30% at the open on the news that the company had received a buy-out offer from Kraft Foods. There is little that the trader could have done to avoid this gap other than having guaranteed the stop order (if possible) in the first place.

The Spread Bettor

Given the price chart in Figure 16 you might think that a spread bettor is immune from gaps, at least on major indices, but this is not necessarily the case. Even spread traders have some non-trading hours and prices can also move up or down suddenly at any time – when foreign markets open (e.g. in New York at 2.30pm UK time), on breaking news during trading hours (e.g. when the Bank of England announces an unexpected 1.5 point interest rate cut), or when a big player makes a large acquisition or disposal.

Often the price spike will be over in a flash, but the spread bettor could still get spiked in or out of a position anyway – at an unfavourable price. It has happened to me, and it will happen to you.

The spread bettor might pay the additional premium to guarantee his stop level, if the provider allows it. Or, as a committed *day trader*, he might seek to eliminate the problem completely by never holding a position overnight or around the time that another market opens.

This implies a very short-term trading style in which he would seek to make several profitable trades per day rather than a single large profit in the course of a week, month, year or decade. It works for some people, some of the time, but it places you at a very real risk of *over-trading*.

The Over-Trader

This trader can turn on a dime, or so he thinks. He uses a clever combination of:

1. A very tight **trailing stop order to sell**, which sells out his position at the very first sign of trouble.

2. A tight **trailing stop order to buy**, which buys him back in again if the downward spike turns out to be temporary and the price recovers.

Sometimes this works, in an orderly market. But when volatility increases, something very curious can happen. The selling price can gap down at the same time that the buying price gaps up. In common parlance, the spread has widened. Which means that his two orders can trigger almost simultaneously: selling him out at an unfavourable price and almost immediately buying him back in at an unfavourable price. At a stroke, he has sold low and bought high.

Even in the normal course of events – without gaps – price slippage can occur in fast moving markets, such that by the time a stop order has executed, the price has moved on from the price at which the stop order was triggered.

As if it's not bad enough for the spread bettor, the kind of swashbuckling over-trading just described can be positively disastrous for an ordinary equity trader operating through a regular broker account. In addition to losing on the bid-ask spread and the potential slippage, he would also need to factor in two sets of dealing charges (on the sell-out and subsequent buy-in), plus stamp duty for equity trades in the UK.

Collectively, these losses from gapping or fast moving markets are known as *whipsaw losses.*

Whipsaw Losses

Having read the information on stop orders provided by your broker, along with the limited coverage of stop orders in other books, it is very tempting to treat stop orders as a trading panacea or Holy Grail. Taken to its logical conclusion, you might find yourself trying to devise a fully automated trading system in which the opening and closing of your positions is driven entirely by stop orders without conscious effort on your part.

It all seems perfectly logical:

- A **stop order to buy** gets you in to a rising trend.

- A **stop order to sell** gets you out of a falling trend.

- The more often you can buy in to a rising trend and sell out of a falling trend, the more money you will make.

You will find yourself subconsciously willing yourself to get stopped out of positions, because – after all – it's good to *cut your losses*. You will think that the more often you can cut a loss by getting stopped out, the better.

This is the road to over-trading and whipsaw losses. I know, because I've been there. It's one of the most valuable lessons I ever learned at the *Investment School of Hard Knocks*.

> The Investment School of Hard Knocks is not a real school. It's my name for the collective losses I made as a *student of the markets*. Many successful traders regard such early losses as the *cost of their trading education*, hence the school analogy.

As described in the previous section, when markets move rapidly down and up and down and up again (you get the idea) an over-trader who tries to catch every twist and turn is likely to lose money on every twist and turn. You can avoid these whipsaw losses by forgetting about **guaranteed stops** and **stops-with-limits** altogether, and simply widen your stops so as to catch the *major* turning points and ignore the minor 'market noise' gyrations.

As legendary investor Jesse Livermore said:

Disregarding the big swing and trying to jump in and out was fatal to me. Nobody can catch all the fluctuations. In a bull market your game is to buy and hold until you believe that the bull market is near its end.

Reminiscences of a Stock Operator *by Edwin Lefèvre*

So while it's good to *cut your losses*, this should not be seen as an aim in itself. As a position trader, my aim is to hold on to positions for as long as I can. The longer you can hold a position:

- The less you will lose in dealing charges, bid-ask spreads and other whipsaw losses.

- The more you will collect in dividends on equity and index positions.

- The less trading work you will have to do; so you can hold down a job, or take a holiday.

So how do we reconcile the two views: that it's good to cut losses (using tight stops) yet preferable to hold positions for as long as possible?

One way is to forget about *cutting losses*, and to think instead about *limiting losses* through a combination of stop orders and position sizing. This subject will be covered in Chapter 11, but in the meantime all this talk of price gaps and whipsaw losses might leave you wondering...

Is the market out to get me?

Like me, you might find yourself from time to time thinking "this market is out to get me". But you'll remember that the majority of trading and investment books you have read advise that the market is not out to get you at all; it has no knowledge of you and is totally neutral towards you.

However, I've learnt from experience that in one sense the market may well be out to get you, and it's related to the issues discussed in this chapter.

Have you noticed that as soon as you get stopped out of (or in to) a position, the price immediately reverses, thus undoing your stop's good work? Well, you might not be imagining it after all.

If you set a **stop order to sell** at, or immediately below, an obvious support level, you may find that you get stopped out more often than you would expect by mere chance. Market makers and other significant market players know that a large number of traders will place **stop-loss orders** at obvious support levels, and they might be motivated to force the price down just that little bit further so as to trigger your – and all the other traders' – stops. Your loss will be their gain as they take over the long positions that you have relinquished, and leave you on the sidelines as the price rises back to its natural level.

The same is also true of the **stop order to buy**. If you place one at, or slightly above, the most recent resistance level – as many people do – you may find yourself at the mercy of those market participants who expect this behaviour from inexperienced traders, or who can even see those orders in the market.

So when deciding where to place a stop order (next chapter) it could be beneficial to choose a non-obvious level: not too close to the most recent support or resistance level; or in line with the last-but-one support or resistance.

Order Execution

Even if the market is not consciously out to get you, you will find that unless you guarantee them, your stop orders will not always execute at the price you specified. This may be outside of the control of your broker, who will only be able to execute your order at the next available market price for your order size *after your stop order has triggered*.

This is why stop orders are said to *guarantee execution, but not price*.

For the exact details of the prices that your broker will respect (*market price* or *their price*), and for details of how they will respond to price gaps and out-of-hours price movements, you will need to refer to their individual terms and conditions. They will have a stated policy on order execution, which is likely to include variations of the following clauses:

- During the hours when [Broker Name] does not offer a service, no stops or orders of any kind will be activated. Upon the opening of any market quoted by [Broker Name] any currently actionable stop order will be filled at the first quote for the relevant market that [Broker Name] are reasonably able to obtain in the market for the size of the order in question.

- If the relevant market is open and trades through or has opened through the level of an order, commonly known as gapping, such order will be executed at the [Broker Name] quote based upon the first price [Broker Name] are reasonably able to obtain in the market.

- In respect of markets quoted by [Broker Name] outside of the trading hours of the relevant market (for example the FTSE 100 trading in US hours), orders may be filled at a price which in our opinion is reasonable in the light of prevailing world markets at the time.

By accepting the broker's terms and conditions you are acknowledging that you are aware of the risks involved in non-guaranteed stops. Rest assured that where your broker provides guaranteed stops (for an additional fee) they will be executed at the agreed level regardless of any gapping or trading hours.

When opening a new position I routinely establish the position with two different brokers or spread betting providers and allocate half of my risk capital to each of them. In part this is to spread my risk of getting stopped-out on a market maker's whim, and in part to gain an insight into which of the brokers is more likely to let this happen.

Author's Avoidance of Price Gaps and Whipsaw Losses

I learned the hard way about leaving tight stops in play overnight, over a weekend or over key news announcements, thereby leaving me at the mercy of price gaps. I don't do this anymore; mainly because I do not set stops too tight (next chapter), or – if I am ever tempted to day trade – by not leaving positions with tight stops open at dangerous times. Although I utilised mandatory **guaranteed stop orders** initially in a 'limited' spread betting account, I nowadays tend *not* to use **guaranteed stops** or **stops-with-limits** because these are not supported consistently across all of the platforms and financial instruments that I trade.

I also learned the hard way about the whipsaw losses that can mount up through over-trading, and in that respect the over-trader example given earlier is more than a little semi-autobiographical. I really did believe that any stop-out was a good stop-out, because 'cutting a loss' was surely *always* a good thing. Yes I was positively willing myself to get stopped out, but now I know better.

And finally, I should remind you that price gaps can adversely affect you at trade entry (when a long trader *buys* or a short trader *sells*) as well as at exit. For this reason, I tend to use mental stops for trade entries on tight stops and I execute these stops manually at the market price – or not, if the price has gapped. I would consider using automatic stops or trailing stops for entry when utilising wide stops to enter long-term investments, since in these cases any price gap is likely to be negligible in the grand scheme of things.

Key Points

- Price gaps are the biggest threat to traders who utilise stop orders.

- Utilising non-guaranteed tight stops can (will) result in over-trading and whipsaw losses.

- Stop orders may not execute at the price you specify.

10

Stop Placement

As illustrated in the previous chapter, there is a fine line to tread between:

1. setting a stop order close enough to the prevailing price that it keeps your potential loss to an absolute minimum, and

2. not setting a stop order so close that it triggers so quickly – and often – that you suffer whipsaw losses and frequently find yourself out of position.

In this chapter I'll look at methods for determining where to place stops.

Stop Distances based on Fixed Percentages

One of the most asked, and least well answered, questions is:

Where should I set my stop level?

It's the least well answered question because there is no simple one-size fits all answer. It's not simply a matter of saying that stop loss orders should be placed at 5%, or 20%, or at any other distance below (for a stop order to sell) or above (for a stop order to buy) the market price.

To illustrate this point I'll draw on the results of a back-testing experiment that I carried out in my book *Financial Trading Patterns*.

Back Testing Trailing Stops for Index Investors

Using historic FTSE 100 index daily closing prices over a number of years I tested the performance of a combined **trailing stop buy / trailing stop sell** pattern using various stop distances. I chose this particular pattern because it lends itself to fully automated back testing using simple rules like "Buy when the index rises by 5% from any minimum and sell when it falls by 10% from any maximum, then repeat". No human interpretation of charts or analysis of fundamentals is required at all; a computer program can be written to run the various scenarios over various time periods using various stop distances.

My back testing program operated using the following rules:

1. Trail the market down until it turns up by the Trailing Stop BUY Distance.

2. Buy in to the market at that price using all available funds.

3. Trail the market up until it turns down by the Trailing Stop SELL Distance.

4. Sell out at that price and bank the proceeds, thereby increasing (hopefully) or decreasing (hopefully not) the available funds.

5. Return to Step 1.

The results of my experiment over two different time periods (23.6 years vs. 8.8 years) using two different stop distance settings (buy at +1% / sell at -10% vs. buy at +20% / sell at -10%) are summarised in the following table.

Time Period	Years	Trailing Stop BUY Distance	Trailing Stop SELL Distance	Absolute Returns	Relative Returns
2nd April 1984 to 28 October 2007	23.6	1%	10%	600%	8%
4th January 1999 to 28 October 2007	8.8	1%	10%	700%	25%
4th January 1999 to 28 October 2007	8.8	20%	10%	860%	48%
2nd April 1984 to 28 October 2007	23.6	20%	10%	200%	-54%

While this table is insufficient in itself to prove that market timing using trailing stops consistently outperforms or underperforms a basic buy-and-hold strategy, it is sufficient in proving that:

- The effectiveness of a *fully automated* market timing strategy using trailing stops is highly sensitive to the chosen stop distances, but in a non-obvious way. In the shorter 8.8 year time period this strategy could outperform a basic buy-and-hold approach by 25% or by 48% depending on the choice of stop distances. In the longer time period this strategy could outperform the basic buy-and-hold strategy by a negligible 8% or underperform by a whopping 54%. We cannot say that tighter stop distances are more effective than wider stop distances over all time periods.

- The effectiveness of a *fully automated* market timing strategy using trailing stops is highly sensitive to the chosen time period. Not merely in terms of *length of time* (8.8 years or 23.6 years), but also in terms of which 8.8 years or which 23.6 years. The shorter period from 1999 to 2007 was chosen specifically as an example of a V-shape bear market followed by bull market, which should be (and turned out to be) ideal conditions for the trailing stop strategy. Hindsight is a wonderful thing, and we could not have known in advance that this would turn out to be an ideal time.

In a nutshell I am saying that it is incredibly difficult, if not impossible, to determine a percentage stop distance or set of stop distances in advance that will perform consistently well under all past, present and future market conditions. All is not lost for stop orders, it just means that we cannot devise a simple, fully-automated trading system based on the application of trailing stop orders with one-size-fits all stop distances. We need to be a lot cleverer and more flexible than that. We need to determine stop distances that are appropriate to market conditions *at the time we place them.*

If the subject of automated trading systems using predefined stop distances does interest you, you will find more back testing results in Michael Covel's book *Trend Following: How Great Traders Make Millions in Up or Down Markets.* In particular he shows how a trading system's drawdown – the maximum interim portfolio depreciation – is affected by setting stop orders at various percentage distances.

Stop Distances based on Volatility

The main problem with trying to determine one-size fits all stop distances for entries and exits in and out of all markets under all timeframes is that this approach takes no account of *volatility* – how much the price of a financial instrument moves up and down day-to-day *normally*, or at least *recently*. If a financial instrument routinely oscillates by 10% over a few days, there's no point setting a protective stop order at minus 2% unless you want to be stopped out often.

There are several methods for determining a financial instrument's volatility and for setting your stop level, or more likely your stop distance (for trailing stop), accordingly. We will now look at some of those methods.

> Keep in mind the fact that while some of these techniques require some hardcore maths, your trading software or brokers website may well provide charts that show volatility indicators.

Beta Adjusted Trailing Stop (BATS)

In an article[2] in *Stocks, Futures and Options* (SFO) magazine, Thomas Bulkowski describes the idea of Beta Adjusted Trailing Stops (BATS). This 2007 article is a rehash of Bulkowski's earlier article in the January 1997 issue of *Technical Analysis of Stocks & Commodities* magazine, in which he cites the Dun and Bradstreet *Guide to Your Investments* as his original source of inspiration.

The *beta* coefficient is a measure of a security's volatility relative to the volatility of the market as a whole; with a beta of 1 meaning that a security is exactly as volatile as the market, a beta of less than 1 meaning that the stock is less volatile than the market, and a beta of more than 1 meaning that the stock is more volatile than the general market. The mathematicians among you can find out more about calculating beta on the Wikipedia page[3], or you can simply rely on the stock price beta values provided by numerous websites such as

---

[2] http://www.sfomag.com/homefeaturedetail.asp?ID=2036152704&MonthNameID=January&YearID=2007

[3] http://en.wikipedia.org/wiki/Beta_(finance)

Yahoo! Finance.

In his article Thomas provides a handy table (based on his research and back testing results) that suggests a trailing stop distance for various combinations of *beta* and *price*. According to this table:

- A higher value of beta necessitates a wider stop distance, so as to not get stopped out due to the high volatility.

- A lower price necessitates a wider stop distance, on the basis that low priced stocks are more volatile.

By way of a concrete example, the suggested trailing stop distance for a stock priced over $50 and having beta 1.01-1.20 is 11%; this is also the suggested trailing stop distance for a stock priced at $0 = $10 where the beta is 0.61 to 0.8.

Be careful about how you interpret the second point listed above, because there is no logical reason why a low priced stock should be more volatile than a different stock with a higher price. But in terms of the same stock: it is true that on its way from $1-per-share to $10-per-share, a $1 movement in price will signify a 100% change at the start of the uptrend (from $1 to $2) whereas it will signify only an 11% change at the end of the run (from $9 to $10). So what he is really getting at here is the fact that you can afford to tighten your trailing stop – in percentage terms – as the price rises higher. Now it just so happens that a fixed-distance trailing stop will automatically become tighter in percentage terms as the price rises.

The basic idea of BATS is to set trailing stop distances according to a security's volatility, so that you get stopped out only when the price trend turns against you and not as a result of daily price fluctuations. (This is also true of the other volatility stops that follow.)

Bollinger Bands

You can get a feel for a security's volatility by looking at its price chart (no maths required). In Figure 17 you can see a Randgold Resources ADS (GOLD) price chart over the period January 2007 to June 2008. I have overlaid Bollinger Bands for the first two quarters so as to give an indication of the peak-to-trough price volatility.

> Devised by John Bollinger in the 1980s, Bollinger Bands are a technical trading tool that indicate volatility on a price chart by plotting the standard deviation (a statistical method that can be used to measure volatility) above and below the moving average price. The overlaying of Bollinger Bands onto a price chart is supported by most charting packages and online price charts.

Having observed the price to have oscillated in a range of no more than about 500 points, a position trader or investor establishing a long position in Q3 2007 might set a wide protective **trailing stop loss order** at minus 750 points. His reasoning would be that any fall of more than 750 points from peak-to-trough would fall outside the normal range, and initially the 750-point stop would achieve his money management objective of losing no more than 33% of capital initially on any single investment.

You can see from the subsequent price history that this trader's reasoning would have proven to be sound in this case. The price trended upwards for three quarters, never falling back by more than 750 points from any peak, until mid-March 2008. The final sell-out price of about 4800 netted the trader a profit of about 2500 points, or more than 100% in nine months.

Figure 17: Volatility-based trailing Stop – Randgold Resources ADS (GOLD)

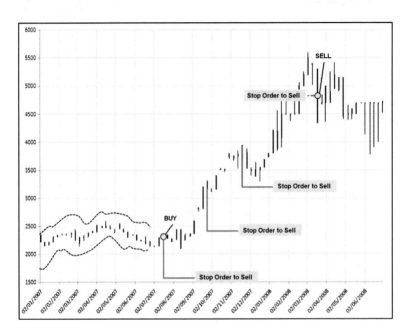

When placing a trailing stop based on recent historic volatility, do keep in mind the fact that as the price gets higher the stop gets tighter. With the price at 2500, the 750-point trailing stop allows for 30% leeway in the price. By the time the price has doubled to 5000, the same 750-point trailing stop allows for only a 15% price drop before being triggered.

Some traders will be happy with this side-effect of trailing stops, on the basis that a stop become less tolerant (therefore keener to crystallise your profits) as the price rises. Others will want to keep the **trailing stop order** in place but adjust the stop distance to 1500 points (back to the original 30%) or in the light of the *changing volatility*.

A note about logarithmic vs. linear scales

In charts that look like the Figure 17, don't be fooled into thinking that a financial instrument has necessarily become more volatile as the price has risen. As just discussed, a 1500-point deviation from a price of 5000 is exactly the same as a 750-point deviation from a price of 2500: in both cases, the same 30% deviation. On linear charts such as the ones used in this book, the price line will look more volatile the further up the scale you go, which is why some traders prefer to look at logarithmic-scale charts that show percentage changes as fixed distances.

> In your charting software package, or on your broker's website, you should be able to alternate between linear and logarithmic scales at the flick of a switch.

Average True Range

Another measure of a financial instrument's volatility is the Average True Range (ATR) devised by J. Welles Wilder.

First you discover the *true range* as a measure of a trading day's price range from the lowest recorded price to the highest recorded price on the day, whether or not these prices correspond with opening or closing prices. And then you average those *true range* values over a number of days, usually 14.

The basic equation for ATR would be:

```
ATR = ( (Day1High - Day1Low) + (Day2High - Day2Low)
+ ... + (Day14High-Day14Low) ) / 14
```

> Note that the time period need not be measured in days; it could be hours, days, weeks, or even months depending on your trading timescale.

Volatility calculation

ATR can be used for a quick calculation of volatility. For example, if a share has a price of 50 and an ATR of 5 then:

Volatility = ATR / price

$$= 5 / 50$$

$$= 10\%$$

Using ATR to determine stops levels

Once you have calculated the ATR over an appropriate period for your target instrument, you set your stop order a multiple of the ATR away from your entry price or from some other chosen price such as the previous day's high or low price. There is no one-size-fits-all multiple, and the optimal value may require some back testing of various multiples on your chosen financial instrument. As a general guide a day trader is likely to set a fractional multiple such as a tight 50% ATR stop or less, a swing trader a 100% ATR stop, and a longer-term position trader or investor would consider a multiple such as 5 x ATR.

Your ATR stop may be implemented as a **trailing stop order** at a distance of 5 x ATR (for example) below the prevailing market price. Alternatively, you might fix a hard non-trailing **stop order** at a level that is 5 x ATR (for example) below your entry price – and then trail it manually or not at all.

All well and good you might think, but there's quite a bit of calculation to do here. The good news is that, as with Bollinger Bands, the charts provided by your trading software or broker's website may well include an ATR indicator such as that shown in Figure 18. The upper pane shows the price of the financial instrument – the EUR/USD spot price in this case – and the lower pane shows the ATR.

Figure 18: EUR/USD Spot with ATR-14

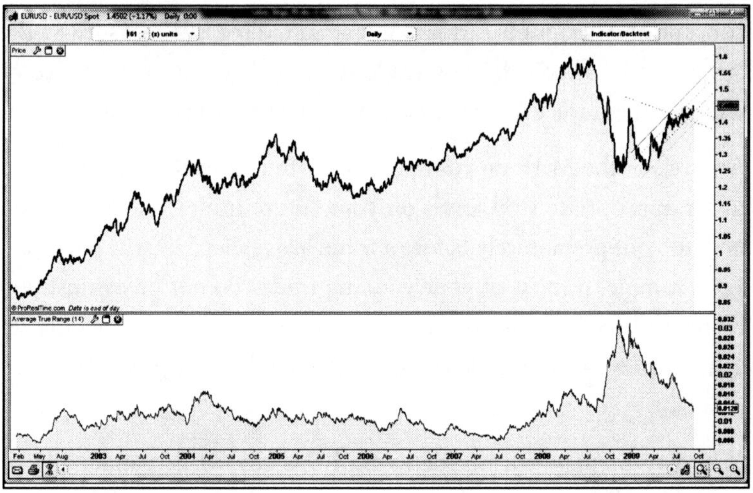

Source: ProRealTime.com

Notice that as the price rises, the ATR stays relatively flat providing the price rise is consistent. And then in late 2008 the ATR shoots up when the price shoots down (i.e. when the volatility increases).

As mentioned above, a short-term trader might set his stop 0.5 x ATR away from the current price, while a long-term investor might set his stop 5 x ATR away from the current price. At the end of the period (shown on the preceding chart) the price was 1.4502 and the ATR was 0.0128.

So (assuming long positions) –

- The *short-term trader* might put a stop order to sell at 1.4502 – (0.5 * 0.0128) = 1.4438

- The *long-term investor* might put a stop order to sell at 1.4502 – (5 * 0.0128) = 1.3862

Maximum Adverse Excursion

Frequent traders who concentrate on one or two markets can use the concept of Maximum Adverse Excursion. This is a measure of the largest loss suffered by any trade while it is open, irrespective of whether the trade eventually closed for a smaller loss or for a profit.

Analysis of the MAE on your previous winning trades may help you to set appropriate stop levels on your future trades, so that you do not stop out prematurely before a trade has realised its true potential. For example, if most of your winning trades do not go against you by more than 25 points on the route into profit, then you would set a **stop order** to cut your losses when those losses are greater than 25 points.

You may or may not decide to trail this stop order; manually or automatically.

Stop Levels based on Support and Resistance

The previous techniques have focused on calculating an appropriate *stop distance* that is *relative* to the trade entry price. Once you have decided on a fixed distance, a BATS distance, a multiple of ATR, or a MAE-based distance, you could – broker permitting – place a **trailing stop order** at the specified distance. In a sense you have used recent historic volatility in order to fix your stop distance (for trailing stops) or stop level (for non-trailing stops) for the life of your trade.

As you learnt in Chapter 8, it is possible – and in some cases necessary – to trail stops manually by adjusting the stop price (always upwards for a long position, never down) *when you consider it prudent to do so.* The phrase "when you consider it prudent to do so" implies a degree of analysis and reflection each time you consider adjusting the stop order.

One such time that you might consider it prudent to adjust a stop order is when you have witnessed the establishment and subsequent testing of a support level (for a long trader) or a resistance level (for a short trader).

- A **support level** is the level at which a falling price is more likely to rebound upwards rather than continue falling. It is the level at which the falling price finds support in the market; it is deemed to be more credible if the price rebounds from this level more than once.

- A **resistance level** is the level at which a rising price is more likely to rebound downwards rather than continue rising. It is the level at which the rising price finds resistance in the market; it is deemed to be more credible if the price rebounds from this level more than once.

If the technical analysis terms support and resistance are unfamiliar enough to require further explanation, you could check out Michael Kahn's book *A Beginner's Guide to Charting Financial Markets.*

Figure 19 shows the price history of Enterprise Inns during 20 March 2009 to 20 April 2009. A trader who establish a position on 27 March at a level of 58 initially places a **stop loss order** at an appropriate distance below based on recent volatility. This example differs from the previous one because the stop order is *not an automated trailing stop*. The stop level does not change at all unless the trader manually changes it; which he does only when the price retraces and then bounces off a notional support level at around 80 on 7 / 8 April. Having witnessed this support level, the trader adjusts the stop level to 75 so as to lie just below the support level. The logic here is that if the price falls through the support level, it indicates a significant change in sentiment from bullish to bearish on this stock.

The price does not fall through the support level, and instead rises to what appears to be a new support level at around 95 on 14 April. The trader adjusts the stop level to 90, thus assuring at least a 32-point profit while letting the profit continue to run.

Note that if the original volatility-based fixed-distance stop order had been trailed upwards automatically, this would certainly have stopped out on 7 April at around the 90 level. This would still have been a healthy profit of 32 points (about 55%) in less than two weeks, but crystallised too soon and thereby not realising the full profit potential of the trade.

Figure 19: Stops based on support levels – Enterprise Inns

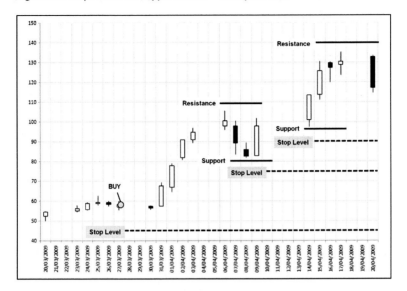

A spread bettor or other long-and-short trader might have been tempted to establish a net short position when stopping out at the 115 level, in order to benefit from what is assumed to be a new downtrend. When setting the stop level for this new short position, the trader would look for a resistance level – above the current price – which should not be penetrated except to indicate a resurgence of the uptrend. Such a resistance level has been observed at just below the 140 level.

> A long trader's resistance level is a short trader's support level, and vice versa.

Trading Timescales

When considering the placement of stop orders based on technical analysis (i.e. price volatility or observed support and resistance levels), it is important to be mindful of your trading timescale.

As a day trader you will be interested in volatility over the preceding minutes and hours, as a swing trader you may be interested in volatility over recent days, and as a position trader or investor you may be interested in volatility over weeks, months or even years. It's the same with support and resistance, which can be observed at different levels *for the same financial instrument* depending on the timescale of the chart you look at.

Figure 20 and Figure 21 show charts for exactly the same financial instrument (it doesn't matter which one – it could be any index, equity or commodity) over a thirteen-year time period between 1996 and 2009, and over a six-week period from May to June 2009, respectively.

The first chart suggests a trading range (an informal measure of volatility) of some 3500 points with long-term support at around 3500 and long-term resistance at around 7000.

Figure 20: Thirteen–Year Volatility

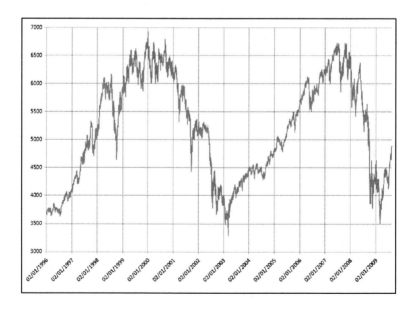

The second chart shows a trading range, which is not even visible on the first chart, of some 200 points with medium-term support at around 4300 and medium-term resistance at around 4500.

Figure 21: Six-Week Volatility (same financial instrument)

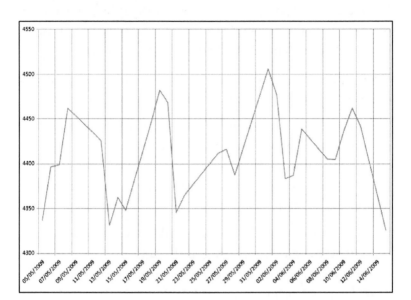

The trader who places stop orders according to the first chart will be looking to trade infrequently for large gains on major trends, and/or will be mindful of getting out of the market "if the worst happens" and the price falls below the 3000 level. The trader who places stop orders according to the second chart will be looking to notch up a quicker, smaller win, or a series of such wins in the form of swing trades.

The first trader would derive little or no benefit from the second chart, and vice versa.

Money Management vs. Trading Characteristics

Some stop placement methods are driven by money management requirements (e.g. the desire to cut losses quickly and to let profits run in order). For example, a trader may implement a stop loss 5% below the current price, because 5% is all he is willing to risk on the trade – the 5% is determined by how much he is willing to lose, not by any reference to the characteristics of the share price.

While other methods are driven purely by reference to the characteristics of the share price (often using price charts).

The *(trailing) stops distances based on fixed percentages* was predominantly a money management technique, whereas the *stop distances based on volatility* and *stop levels based on support and resistance* were more sympathetic to the trading characteristics of the securities in question.

The trick is to place stops at levels that take into account the trading characteristics of a security while at the same time achieving your overall money management objectives. Your stop placement policy might be something like this:

I will place a stop order just below the most recent support level (*trading characteristics*) that is no more than 20% below the current price (*money management*).

Where I say "just below the most recent support level" you may take this informally, or more formally in terms of the volatility indicators discussed earlier. In the latter case you might rephrase the first part of your stop placement policy as:

I will place a stop order at 0.5 * ATR below the most recent support level that is no more than 20% below the current market price.

Your stop placement may also be a function of your anticipated reward-risk ratio.

A wide 20% protective stop on a long-term position trade or investment gives a massive reward-risk ratio of 45:1 if you are anticipating the investment to become a ten-bagger over time. In this happy scenario your £1000 investment could yield a £9000 profit at the risk of losing only £200.

Over a much shorter timescale, day traders like Nick McDonald [see Chapter 14] consider the reward-risk ratio – and place their stops accordingly – on every trade. In this respect, volatility measures such as ATR may be useful in gauging the upside potential of a trade (more volatility means more potential profit) as well as the downside potential (the likelihood of getting stopped out for a given loss) so that stop-loss orders can be placed for an acceptable trade-off between risk and reward.

Not Just "Stopping Out"

The prior discussions in this chapter have focused mainly on the placement of stop orders to close out long positions. This will be the most common use of stop orders, but is not the only use. Don't forget that a long trader may also use a **stop order to buy** in order to *enter a new long position.*

Breakout Stop Placement for Trade Entry

One of the most inspirational trading stories is that of Nicolas Darvas, a professional-dancer-turned-trader who made $2 million from stock market investments in the 1950s. It was a lot of money back then (and come to think of it – it still is!)

Darvas devised a system whereby he would identify a stock's price oscillating within a box on a chart. When the price broke upwards out of one box and into another box he considered this to be a buy signal. It's a variation of the technique we now know as buying on breakout, and one that is ideally suited to the application of stop orders.

A long trader will often place a **stop order to buy** at a level above the resistance level that defines the top of an established trading range, so as to enter a position when the price breaks upwards out of the range. Once again, an appreciation of a security's volatility will be useful in determining exactly where to place the stop order, as there's no point using a stop order to enter a new position at a price within the normal volatile range.

Traders who place a **stop order to buy** at exactly, or just above, a resistance level should be aware that market makers and other market participants will know this. As will be explained later in this chapter, your opponents – for that's what they are – may well be motivated to ramp the price to trigger all the stops placed near the resistance level before allowing the price to fall back to its previous level. To make matters worse, this may be a psychological trick designed to frighten you into closing your newly-opened position immediately – just before the price really does break upwards and you have no open position from which to benefit.

Always remember that –

Scared money never wins!

For all traders, other than ultra-short-term day traders, it may be useful to set your stop order to buy at what you consider – by trial and error, but read on – to be a safe distance above the resistance level, so that you buy in only if the price truly breaks out of the prior range. And don't assume too soon that the old resistance level has become a new support level below which the price cannot fall at least temporarily. Better to set your subsequent protective **stop order to sell** at a level below the support level of the original trading range.

Trailing Stop Placement for Trade Entry

An alternative approach to (long) trade entry is that of trailing a **stop order to buy** downwards so as to buy in ultimately at a more attractive (lower) price. Unlike a **limit order**, which would execute at a level that you presupposed would be the low point, and while the price was still moving downwards, your **trailing stop order** would not require you to guess the low point in advance and would execute only when the price started to rise.

Broker permitting, the order can be trailed automatically, but beware that an automatically-adjusted stop level will not correspond with any established resistance levels and will trigger simply when the price turns upwards by a specified amount.

Also be careful to place a protective **stop order to sell** as soon as the **stop order to buy** is executed, just in case the price resumes its previous downward trend.

Swing Trading Stop Placement for Trade Entry

The breakout stop placement for trade entry implies that you will profit from the fact that a price that breaks upwards from a trading range will continue to rise; at least for a short time if you're a day trader, and hopefully as part of a longer-term uptrend if you are a trend-following position trader. The trailing stop placement for trade entry implies that as a position trader or investor you will profit as a result of buying in to a new rising trend at a low price.

But when and where would a swing trader place his or her stops?

As indicated in Chapter 8, a swing trader is perhaps more likely to use a **limit order to buy** at the bottom of a trading range, and a **limit order to sell** at the top of a trading range, thereby relegating the stop order to the role of protection against getting it wrong.

And yet there may be another role for stop orders in swing trade entry.

If you are able to monitor your target instrument with appropriate frequency – constantly for an intra-day swing trade, or less frequently for an inter-day swing trade – you need not place limit orders for entry at all.

When the price falls to the bottom of the established trading range you place a **stop order to buy** at a few points above the current market price, and a **stop order to sell** at a few points below the current market price.

The price will now do one of three things:

- The price will rebound upwards as expected, in which case the **stop order to buy** will establish a long position for the swing trade.

- The price will rebound falsely and then fall, so that the **stop order to buy** will establish a long position and the protective **stop order to sell** will shortly afterwards close the position for a small loss (but beware notching up too many whipsaw losses in this way).

- The price will fall right through the bottom of the trading range without rebounding at all, in which case the **stop order to sell** will establish a new short position in anticipation of a downtrend (so only take this approach if you are indifferent as to whether you will swing trade or trend-trade on a breakout).

Stop placement for short traders

For clarity and consistency, much of the prior discussion has focused on how – and where – a long trader will place a **stop order to buy** for trade entry and a **stop order to sell** for trade exit. These discussions are just as relevant to the short trader who will use stop orders in the opposite sense: a **stop order to buy** placed at an appropriate level to *exit an existing position*, and a **stop order to sell** placed at an appropriate level to *enter a new position*.

In one sense the long trader's support level is the short trader's resistance level, and vice versa, but this need not concern us because long traders and short traders would both place a **stop order to buy** above a resistance level and a **stop order to sell** below a support level.

Beware Dividends on Equity Positions

You might be surprised to hear me advising you to be wary of dividend payments on your equity positions.

Didn't you invest in order to collect those very dividends?

Yes, but there is a potential problem in relation to the placement of your stop orders. When a 6% dividend becomes payable on a stock or index position, the price will fall by a similar amount to compensate for the fact that new buyers will not be entitled to the dividend. Your stop order at minus 3% could be triggered as a result of the price falling for this purely technical reason, where the real value of your holding has not fallen at all.

The moral of the story is to be aware of the ex dividend dates, and the size of the proposed dividends, for any dividend-paying positions you hold. Immediately prior to the ex dividend date you should ensure that any stop order is sufficiently below the price as to absorb the dividend adjustment.

Beware Obvious Stop Levels

As indicated earlier, one should be wary of placing stop orders at obvious levels.

Victor Sperandeo (Trader Vic) says:

> *Aware of these stop points, the locals as well as the brokers who trade on their own account have a vested interest in driving prices slightly above or below these "resistance" or "support" points to force execution of stop loss orders. This is called "taking out the stops".*
>
> **Trader Vic: Methods of a Wall Street Master**

Having your stops taken out will cause you either to miss the price move that you expected and which resumes as soon as you are taken out, or will force you to re-enter your position at a less favourable price with the added costs of the bid-ask spread and any dealing charges.

Support and resistance levels

The most obvious stop levels are recent support and resistance levels, so it may be wise to set your stops a little further from them than you would do otherwise; or it may be wise to look at the last-but-one levels as less obvious candidates. There is no perfect answer here that will protect you from having your stops taken out occasionally. Trial and error is required here (and if you do find the perfect answer – don't tell anyone!)

Figure 22 gives an example in which the price spikes down briefly below a support level before embarking on a significant uptrend. A trader who observed the price chart for Sports Direct during July and August 2009 may have identified support at around 82 and may therefore have placed a tight stop at 2.5% below this level (i.e. at 80). On 4 September the price spiked down briefly to touch this level, thus taking out his stop, before embarking on a significant uptrend. We can only speculate as to what caused this suspicious price behaviour.

Figure 22: Spike Down before Trend Up on Sports Direct

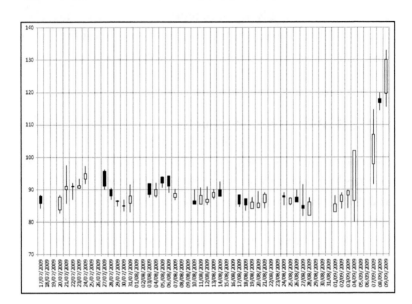

Round numbers

Beware also round numbers. The market makers and other professional participants know that amateur traders tend to set stops at (or very close) to psychological boundaries, such as 5000 on the FTSE 100 index. It should be obvious that a price of 5000 is psychologically more significant than a price of 4500, which in turn is more significant than a price of 4550; but this very much depends on the timescale you are trading – to a day trader, the 4550 could be very significant!

There's no magic formula for this, but as a general rule: the higher the number, and the longer your trading timescale, the further from the round number your stop should be. So whereas a day trader might place a stop at least 5 points away from the 4550 level, a position trader would be better advised to place a stop at least 50 points away from the 5000 level.

On the face of it, it seems that the **automated trailing stop** avoids the issue of obvious stop levels entirely. Your stop order at a distance of 10 points below the prevailing market price will trail through many non-obvious levels as the price rises. But do keep in mind that the professionals know that amateur traders have a tendency to trail stops at a round number of points (or percentage) distance from the market price. They may be ready to stop you out when the price falls by exactly 10 points from any high, or by exactly 10%, so try setting your stop distance at 11 points or maybe at 13%.

There is no foolproof rule on this issue. If I were to tell you that a stop distance of 13% was a safe bet, and if enough readers took me up on this suggestion, then it could become the new (known to everyone) norm.

More about Market Makers

Market makers are intermediaries who provide liquidity in the market. Rather like a car dealer who will always offer to sell you a car or buy a car from you, to save you having to find your own private buyer or seller, a market maker stands ready to buy or sell illiquid securities at a moment's notice *whenever you wish to trade.*

Just like the car dealer, the market maker will offer you a lower price (sometimes much lower) to buy what you want to sell, and will ask for a higher price (sometimes much higher) to sell what you want to buy. The difference between these two prices is called the *spread*, which will widen or narrow according to the margin of safety that the market maker deems necessary. When there are large numbers of equally-matched buyers and sellers for a given security, the market maker can buy shares and then sell them on immediately without building an excessive premium into the spread.

For less-frequently-traded securities, the market maker may have to buy shares from you (as he is obliged to do) and hold them in stock until a buyer can be found. Similarly, when you want to buy an illiquid security, it is useful for the market maker to have some 'in stock' so as not to have to find a seller at short notice. Just as the car dealer has to manage his stock levels, so does the market maker. Sometimes he will have excess inventory that he needs to offload, and sometimes he will not be able to stock up quickly enough.

It is unlikely that you will ever deal with a market maker directly, other than behind the scenes via your retail broker, but an appreciation of who they are and how they work is useful in deducing how – and why – stop orders at obvious levels are prone to being *stopped out*.

Here is a theoretical example:

Suppose a stock has dropped down to $10 four times and each time bounced back up, thus establishing an identifiable (on a chart) resistance level. Many traders will place their stop orders just below this level, say at $9.90. Since the market makers can either see those orders in the market, or in any case can assume their presence from experience, they can simply drop their quoted price down to $9.90 so as to trigger the stops.

It's not just market makers or other traders who will target your stop orders, you might be pitting your wits against a computer...

Computer algorithms

In the modern computer-driven world there are automatic algorithms (i.e. computer programs) that have been designed to seek out traders' stop levels, with a view to ramping prices up or down when trading volumes are low so as to "take out" (trigger) the stops. Some traders refer to these algorithms by informal names like 'ping' or 'plunge' (probably not the real names) according to the way they are perceived to work. It is because of the presence of these algorithms specifically in equity markets that some traders have moved away from day-trading stocks – preferring instead to position trade or to trade other non-equity markets.

Taking on the Market Makers (and other professionals)

There are a few ways in which you can counter the threat just outlined. None of these remedies is perfect, but you might consider:

- Using mental stops. This will obviously prevent your stop orders from being visible to other parties, but of course will not prevent experienced professionals from guessing the levels at which your stops are likely to be set. And the problem of mental stops is that you must be ready and willing to execute them yourself when the time comes. This remedy may be appropriate for day traders who hold few positions open simultaneously.

- Access Level 2 data that shows you the queued buy and sell orders in the system, just like the market makers can. This will provide you with a deeper insight into the likely (short-term) price action. Your broker may provide this data free if you trade frequently on their advanced trading platform, or you may be able to subscribe for a monthly fee. Again, this remedy may be more useful to short-term traders.

- Trade highly liquid securities, and not shares of smaller companies for whom there are few – and possibly only one – market maker. Although this remedy is applicable to all trading timescales, it is no accident that day traders who use very tight stops often choose to trade foreign exchange – by far the largest and most liquid market in the world.

For longer-term position traders and investors the issue of price manipulation may be of little or no significance, and may not be worth getting paranoid about. By holding liquid securities (e.g. bigger companies) with wide protective stops, you are already protected from short-term price manipulations on illiquid securities. You will probably never even notice.

Don't Forget The Spread!

When deciding on an appropriate stop level or distance, it is very easy to do so with reference to the mid-price shown on a price chart, with no accounting for the bid-ask spread. I've done this, and so will you.

If you are trading small-cap illiquid stocks rather than blue-chip stocks, or spread bets rather than CFDs, you must also account for the wider spread by adding at least half of it on to your stop distance. Otherwise, the stop order that you thought would trigger when the price fell to 195 might actually trigger when the price chart shows 200 for the stock that has a bid-ask spread of 195-205.

Stop Placement for Long-Term Investors

Long-term investors who buy shares or commodities when they consider them to be undervalued on some fundamental measure, and then sell them when they are overvalued by the same measure, may be left a little dazed and confused by the discussions of stop placement in this chapter.

Relax! You are most likely to enter and exit positions manually at the market price when you consider your entry or exit criteria to have been met. In this scenario your use of stop orders will be restricted to an if-all-else-fails safety net, to protect you from the worst ravages of the market when you are not watching. As such, you might simply place a **stop order to sell** at a level that is 20% below your entry price – and forget about it. If you think that 20% sounds rather large – because no one wants to lose 20% of their investment – it may be useful to think of this in relation to the anticipated payback. If you invested on the basis that your value stock could double in price, taking your $1000 investment to $2000, then your reward-risk ratio is 5:1. That is, you stand to make $1000 profit by placing only $200 at risk.

Or you might be a little more sophisticated and use a simple combination of factors when placing your stop order. Remember that your stop is less likely to be triggered – and as a long-term investor you really don't want it to be – if it is well outside of normal volatility (say 5xATR below the current price) *as well as* below a significant resistance level. A quick look at the price chart (showing ATR) should tell you what you need to know. Repeat periodically, or set to trail automatically.

Key Points

- Stop orders can be set to trail at a fixed distance from a moving price, they can be placed according to a security's volatility, or they can be adjusted periodically to coincide with support and resistance levels.

- There is a trade-off between tight stops that trigger easily for a small loss (or larger secured profit) vs. wide stops that trigger less easily but for a larger loss (or small secured profit).

- There is a trade-off between setting stops based purely on money management criteria vs. setting them based on the trading characteristics of the security.

- The placement of stop orders will depend on whether they are used to enter or exit a position, and on whether that position is long or short.

- Consider stop placement as a function of risk and reward.

- Beware obvious stop levels.

11

Position Sizing

Apart from stop orders, there is another way to limit your potential loss: don't stake so much in the first place. In this chapter I'll look at limiting losses through effective position sizing, with a view to bringing the two techniques – stop orders and position sizing – together as a combined mechanism for limiting losses.

In simple terms, *position sizing* means how much you invest, or stake, in relation to how much you are prepared to lose.

If you place a £10-per-point spread bet then, compared with a £1-per-point spread bet, you are taking ten times the risk in the hope of making ten times the reward. If you invest $10,000 in a stock that could conceivably go bust then, compared with investing $1,000, you are also taking ten times the risk in the hope of making ten times the reward. If the $10,000 represents your entire life savings you might consider it to be more prudent to take ten $1,000 separate gambles than to risk the whole $10,000 on one spin of the wheel in the Wall Street casino.

The Kelly Formula

While on the subject of casinos you might be interested to know that in the 1950s J. L. Kelly described a formula to determine the optimal size of a series of bets; initially in the context of card playing (see Edward O. Thorpe's book *Beat the Dealer*) and subsequently in the context of financial markets.

The idea is that by betting no more than the amount suggested by the Kelly Formula, you stand the best chance of coming out ahead before you run out of money.

The basic formula (which sources express in slightly different ways) is:

```
Percentage funds to stake = ((odds offered *
probability of win) - probability of loss) / odds
offered
```

So if a casino – or for that matter, a financial broker – offers you odds of 2-1 on a coin toss and you know that the probability of a win is 50%, then:

```
((2 * 0.5) - 0.5%) / 2 = 0.25
```

which means you should stake no more than 25% of your available funds on each bet.

To save you doing the calculations yourself, there are several online Kelly Formula calculators, such as the one at www.albionresearch.com/kelly.

When applied to financial markets, the Kelly Formula is not perfect. Not least because where the odds of losing are so small and the odds winning are so large – think 'value' stocks – the formula would encourage you to stake a large proportion of your available funds (more than 75%) on a single position. For this reason some traders would routinely stake a consistent fraction of the 'Kelly Bet' on each position, for example staking 15% of available funds when the formula suggests 30%.

Those of you who don't want to put blind trust in the Kelly Formula, or who don't want to do the calculations, will be reassured to know that there are other ways to practice position sizing...

Other position sizing techniques

Diversification is a simple form of risk reduction through position sizing. By investing $1,000 in each of ten different stocks you are reducing your risk of a total wipe-out compared with investing $10,000 in one stock.

Dollar (or Pound or Euro) Cost Averaging is another form of risk reduction through position sizing. By investing $1,000 each month in a Dow Jones index tracking fund you are reducing your risk of investing the whole amount at the worst possible time. Note that dollar cost averaging does not reduce your risk of a total wipe-out if you average down on one stock, so it is better practised using an index fund such as an exchange traded fund.

A more advanced form of position sizing would involve investing an amount relative to how far the price of a stock or an index has fallen from its all-time high: if the FTSE 100 index has fallen by 10% you might invest 10% of your available funds; if the FTSE index has fallen 30% you might invest 30% of your available funds. Whereas, as a momentum investor, you might do the exact opposite: commit additional funds as the price of a stock, index or commodity rises.

Yet another form of position sizing would involve placing a higher £-per-point spread bet on a stock whose fundamentals – P/E, PEG, or Dividend Yield – look attractive than on a stock which you regard as a pure gamble. Your position size is related to your level of confidence.

This is not meant to be an exhaustive list of position sizing techniques, but merely an indication of how you might control your risk by deciding how much to invest (or bet) – and when. Your position size determines how much you could lose, and should be prepared to lose, in the absence of a stop order.

Using Stop Orders and Position Sizing together

One of the problems of using position sizing alone to limit your downside risk is that it also limits your upside potential; which goes against –

Minor Axiom I : Always play for meaningful stakes

as documented by Max Gunther in his book *The Zurich Axioms*. Too small a position size (not a meaningful stake) will yield too small a profit. One way around this problem is to use position sizing in conjunction with a stop order.

A position size of $10,000 with no stop loss places $10,000 of your money at risk. In contrast, a position size of $100,000 with a **stop loss order** at -10% places the same $10,000 at risk (assuming that the stop loss is guaranteed). The upside potential is greater in the latter case because a $100,000 position size will yield ten times as much profit – as an absolute amount of money, not as a percentage – compared with the $10,000 investment.

The key point here is that you can take the same risk by investing a smaller amount (smaller position size) with a wider stop or no stop at all, or by investing a larger amount (bigger position size) with a tighter stop.

Taken to its logical conclusion, one would be tempted to invest a considerably greater amount of $1,000,000 with a **stop loss order** at -1%. But there are some problems.

One problem is that most likely you will not have $1,000,000 of investment funds in ready cash, although *theoretically* a spread bettor could establish a $1,000,000 position with a lower initial stake – thanks to the leveraged nature of spread bets.

The more relevant problem is that the tighter your stop distance, the more likely you are to get stopped out of your position. As you have learnt in this chapter and the previous one, getting stopped out frequently gives you more work to do (in establishing new positions) and it generates whipsaw losses (as a result of dealing charges, the bid-ask spread, and any trading taxes such as stamp duty).

How much can you afford to lose?

The trick is to determine how much you can stand to lose on each trade, and to limit your loss through a combination of effective position sizing and the application of a **stop loss order** at an appropriate distance.

If your acceptable level of loss on any trade is $500, and your chosen security or other financial instrument has volatility of 4% (for example an ATR of 0.8 against a current price of 20), then a position size of $10,000 with a **stop loss order** at -5% would seem to be an acceptable trade-off between position size and stop level.

Using Stops to Increase Trading and Investment Funds

As you have seen; by applying (or tightening) a stop order, you can decrease your level of risk for a given position size. Now let's turn this idea on its head. By tightening a stop order you can increase your position size for a given level of risk.

Suppose you invested $10,000 in a Dow Jones index tracking ETF at the 8000 level with no stop loss. If we assume that the entire index could conceivably fall all the way to zero (however unlikely this is) then your amount at risk would be the full $10,000. If you now set a stop-loss at the 4,000 level, and you assume that it would execute faithfully at this level, then you have effectively reduced your amount at risk to $5,000. Consequently you could afford to invest an additional $5,000 in the same ETF, or in a different ETF or individual stock, in order to bring your overall amount at risk to the original $10,000.

By applying a **stop loss order** when none existed before, you can, in a sense, increase the funds that you have available for investment. This is purely notional in the above example because you still need to find the additional $5,000 for the second investment. You still need $15,000 of total investment funds even though you are risking only $10,000 worth.

> With spread betting things work rather differently. Depending on the margin requirements, the level of your stop loss order, and the algorithm that the spread betting provider uses, you may well find that your *Trading Resources* (or *Total Position* as some spread betting firms call it) really does increase when you tighten your stop orders. More funds are available for you to trade without you necessarily having to deposit additional money.

This side-effect of stop orders allows for a form of pyramiding in which you raise your stop levels in line with rising prices, and then reinvest the notional (as in the ETF example) or real (as in spread betting example) additional funds.

What is your Expectancy?

Once you have sufficient trading history – I'm talking about hundreds of trades, so this might be one for the day traders and swing traders – you can calculate your average effectiveness, or the *expectancy* of your trading strategy.

By analysing your past trades you might discover that 80% of the time your trades get stopped out for a 10% loss (inclusive of trading costs), but 20% of the time you manage to run your profits for a 100% gain (inclusive of trading costs). This would give a positive expectation of 12%, calculated as:

$(.20 * 1) + (.80 * -0.10) = 0.12$

This means that over your trading lifetime you would expect to make an *average* net return of 12% on each trade, despite losing money 80% of the time!

> **!** Note that if your own calculations produce a negative expectation, you cannot possibly hope to win at the trading game over the long term. You should stop trading, or change your strategy!

Your stop distances will affect the expectancy of your trading strategy, because tighter stops will increase the probability of you getting stopped out (for a small loss) whereas wider stops will decrease the probability of getting stopped out (but for a larger loss).

The probabilities used to calculate your trading expectancy should influence your position size. In this example you would on average make 12% on each trade over a large number of trades. But with an 80% failure rate it would not be wise to bet the farm – i.e. 100% of your trading capital – on your very first trade, thereby getting wiped out before you reach the fifth trade that (on average) more than makes up for the previous four losses.

Determination of Stop Distances and Position Sizing

Since I regard myself as predominantly a position trader, I try very hard not to get stopped out. As such I tend to trail my stops up to just below the last-but-one support level, and no closer than 25% below the most recent price peak. In the event that I decided to trail stops entirely automatically – for example if I went on an extended holiday – I would regard 25% as an appropriate stop distance.

When first establishing a position I tend to rely on position sizing (not betting or investing too much) rather than a stop-loss order. Once the position has moved into profit – defined as me being able to place a stop order that would secure a profit – I will consider adding to the position on the next significant dip.

Key Points

- Losses can be limited using position sizing as a complement to using stop orders.

- Effective risk management recognises the interplay between stop orders and position sizing.

12

Perfect Trades

This chapter presents a series of perfect trades – trades that have been, or could have been, enacted in real life; with the application of stop orders having rendered those trades successful. Remember that for a stop order to be considered successful, it could have *let a profit run* or it could have *cut a loss*. So a successful trade need not have closed with a profit. In fact, the first (day trading) example is considered a success by the hypothetical day trader who executes it, despite closing out at a loss. So these perfect trades do not represent absolute perfection, because there is always room for improvement. But each one of them succeeds, or fails gracefully, due to the effective use of stop orders.

The price histories shown in the charts are real price histories for real stocks or other financial instruments; only the personas of the traders and investors in these examples are hypothetical. I have expressed price levels devoid of any currency. The underlying currency may be British pounds, or US dollars or cents, or Euros, it really doesn't matter. An increase in price from 70 to 100 is just as impressive when expressed in any of those currencies.

Whereas the majority of the examples up to this point in the book have focused on the FTSE 100 index for consistency, in this chapter and the next I demonstrate stop orders in the contexts of other markets including individual equities, foreign exchange currency pairs, and international (non-UK) indices.

Perfect Day Trade

Sally is a day trader who operates through a spread betting account. Her perfect day trade is illustrated in Figure 23.

On 3 April 2009 she notices that the share price of Bank of Ireland has risen quickly shortly after the market opens, and she concludes that the price will most likely fall to close the gap. When the price begins to fall, she sells short at 75 and plans to take her 15-point profit if and when the price hits 60, thereby almost closing the gap. She might place a **limit order to buy** for this, not shown. At the time she establishes her short position, she specifies a **stop order to buy** (effectively a stop loss order) at 80, just above the recent price peak, to stop her out at a 5-point loss if she is wrong. Her target reward-risk ratio on any trade is 3:1, and this trade with this stop level meets that criterion.

The subsequent price action in Figure 23 shows that the gap does not close as expected, and so the short position is exited automatically by the **stop loss order to buy**. Although this trade concluded with a loss, it is still considered a *successful trade* because the stop order did its job of limiting the loss to only 5 points. The maximum potential loss on the short position during the day would have risen to more than 15 points, and although the subsequently price fell back to a price of 75, it still failed to close the gap and the next day rose even higher.

Figure 23: Perfect Day Trade – Bank of Ireland

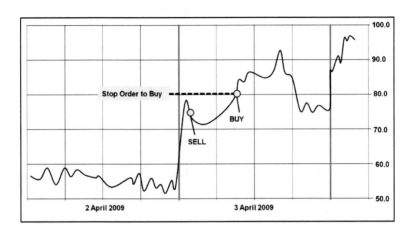

It is also worth noting in this example that another spread bettor, Robbie, who was not a *committed day trader*, might have been tempted to place opposing **stop order to sell** (at 70) and **stop order to buy** (at 80) orders towards the end of the day on 3 April when the price had apparently settled around the 75 level and could go either way the next day. With the price gapping up above 85 on the next trading day following the weekend, this spread bettor would have established a long position at a 5-point disadvantage due to the price gap, unless his **stop order to buy** had been *guaranteed*. Sally-the-day-trader would not have left stop orders open over the weekend at all, or even overnight.

Some readers will observe that had Sally placed a *long spread bet* at 75 instead of the short spread bet, with a stop loss order at 70, she could have held on until 6 April, without being stopped out, for a 20-point profit. But Sally would point out that we only know with hindsight that a long position could have worked out better than a short position; and she would prefer to take a 5-point loss on being wrong – and live to trade another day – than to hold on to a position over the weekend.

This example has demonstrated the successful use of a stop order in the context of a day trader who has established a short position (as a spread bet) with the protection of a stop loss order. Incidentally it has also demonstrated how a spread bettor who is not a day trader would have been foolish to hold a tight stop order over a weekend unless this stop order could be guaranteed.

> Note that although I have used an equity chart in this day trading example, a day trader is just as likely – if not more likely – to be trading currencies because the FOREX market is the largest and most liquid market in the world that can be traded 24-hours-a-day. The principle would be exactly the same as in my example.

Perfect Swing Trade

Jim is a swing trader who trades major indices using exchange traded funds (ETFs). His perfect trade is illustrated in Figure 24.

Late in November 2008 he notices that the FTSE 100 index has bounced off a low point at about 3750, which corresponds almost exactly with a low point the previous month. He recognises this as a support level, so he establishes a long position at 3900 using a FTSE 100 ETF and places a **stop order to sell** at 3600 in case he is wrong. Having witnessed a most recent significant high point at around 4750, he concludes that this might represent a resistance level and therefore places a **limit order to sell** at 4600, which would yield a targeted profit of 700 points (about 18%).

Jim's set-up works perfectly as planned. The price continues to rise, so the protective **stop order to sell** *does not trigger* but the **limit order to sell** *does trigger* thus securing the targeted 700-point profit.

Figure 24: Perfect Swing Trade – FTSE 100 Index

Note that Jim's friend Joe, who is a long-and-short spread bettor, could have established a net short position at this point – with a **stop order to buy** (shown greyed out) as protection against being wrong. Jim himself could have established a short position by *buying a FTSE 100 Short ETF*, with a protective **stop order to sell** (out of his *long* position in the *Short ETF*) corresponding with Joe's protective **stop order to buy** (out of his *short* bet on the FTSE 100 index).

Whether or not Jim attempts to benefit from the downward price swing by going short, he would certainly place a new **limit order to buy** at 3900 so as to buy into another upswing from the support level, with a **stop order to sell** (as before) at 3600 in case the upswing fails to materialise. In the chart, a new upswing does fail to materialise and the new long position is closed with a 300-point loss.

Over the whole cycle, long-only Jim has made a net profit of 700-300 = 400 points, or about 10%. Long-and-short Jim, or his spread-betting friend Joe, could have secured an additional 700-point profit over the cycle.

This example has demonstrated the combined use of **limit orders** and **stop orders** in the context of a long (and potentially short) swing trade with a timescale measured in weeks or months. The trader would have had some idea at the outset as to the timescale for this trade (or these trades).

Perfect Position Trade

Bob is a position trader whose perfect position trade is illustrated in Figure 25.

Having established a position, he will cut his losses if the trade turns against him; and he will run his profits – for as long as he can, but no longer – if it goes the way he planned. He prefers to trade foreign exchange (FOREX) currency pairs via his spread betting account.

At the beginning of 2008 he notices that the Euro (EUR) currency has begun strengthening against the Pound (GBP) after a prior period, longer than shown in the chart, during which the currencies had traded in a tighter range. His assessment is that the Euro will continue to strengthen relative to the Pound, since sterling will suffer more as a result of the unfolding international financial crisis.

In January 2008 he places a GBP/EUR spread bet with a trailing stop order at distance 0.40 below his purchase price. He decided on this distance because it placed the stop order initially at a level just below the support level of the prior trading range. Once decided, he then maintains this fixed stop distance throughout the life of the trade. (If his spread betting provider had not supported trailing stops, he would have been fully committed to trailing the stop manually.)

Sure enough, the Euro continues to strengthen against the pound and the market price rises, with the trailing stop level also rising exactly in line at a fixed distance below. For clarity, the chart shows only the trailing stop adjustments resulting from new price peaks, but in reality there could be many interstitial adjustments. Of most importance is the fact that the stop distance remains constant in this scenario.

The price history peaks at near parity (1 Euro = 1 GBP) and then falls back, triggering the **stop order** at a level of 1 Euro = 0.92 GBP. From the initial level of 1 Euro = 0.73 GBP this represents a 26% increase in one year.

> ! Note that since spread bets are leveraged trades, the actual profit may be much greater than 26% depending on the amount of gearing. The 26% price increase would equate to a 26% profit in a non-leveraged trade.

Figure 25: Perfect Position Trade – GBP / EUR FOREX

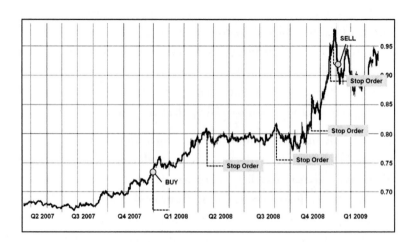

This example demonstrates the use of a trailing stop order in the context of a foreign exchange (FOREX) currency trade. The life of the trade is one year, but this timescale was not set in advance. The trade could have run for as little as a few days or as long as a decade – although the latter timescale is most unlikely.

Perfect Investment

As a serious investor looking to invest a sizable lump sum for retirement, Debbie has a multi-year timeframe and prefers the security of a diversified portfolio to the excitement of speculating on individual stocks. Her perfect investment is illustrated in Figure 26.

After the dot.com crash at the turn of the century, she considers the world's major stock indices to have bottomed-out at the beginning of 2003 and decides to invest her $100,000 'retirement' savings in the S&P 500 index via a traditional mutual fund. Although she has no intention of *cutting her losses* if the fund falls in value, she is determined to lock in a good proportion of any growth that occurs.

Although she sees this as a long-term investment, she is not fooled by the fund salesman's "buy and hold" mantra. She knows that an investment in the S&P 500 in 1997 would have almost doubled by 2000, but then halved again by 2002. It happened then, and it could happen again.

She invests her $100,000 in the first quarter of 2003 at an index level of 825 and with no stop level. She knows that, unlike an individual stock, the level of the S&P 500 cannot conceivably become totally worthless (i.e. go bust). She has a long time horizon and will not need to take back her investment, hence crystallise any loss, at any time before retirement.

The index rises significantly in the course of the 4 to 5 years, falling back occasionally along the way. Each time the index falls back notably, she considers her stop level policy. Each time, she notes that the price has fallen by about 50 points from peak-to-trough, and she places her mental stop at 75 points (which is 1.5 x peak-to-trough range) below the trough.

Note that Debbie is an unsophisticated trader who has no formal understanding of Average True Range (ATR) or other volatility indicators. But in effect she is determining her stop level informally as a multiple of her rough-and-ready volatility assessment (the peak to trough range), in the same way that a more sophisticated trader might determine a stop distance as a multiple of ATR.

Although as a mutual fund investor she cannot place an automated stop order, she is 100% committed to exiting her investment if the index level ever falls to the most recent stop level that she noted. This increasing mental stop level is intended to protect some of her profit in a worst case scenario. In effect she is trailing her stop order, but not in the way that an automated stop order would trail. The effective stop distance will widen as the price rises, before the price corrects and a new stop level is noted.

Debbie really doesn't want to ever get stopped out, and like Warren Buffett she believes that "The best period to hold [a stock] is forever". Hence the wide, and periodically widening, mental stops. All the time that she is holding, she is benefitting from dividend income as well as capital appreciation.

Although she would have preferred not to get stopped out, there comes a time when she has to. Late in 2007 she is disciplined enough to instruct her fund manager to sell out of the S&P 500 mutual fund when the index level falls to her most recent stop level; and it's a good thing too, as you can see in the chart. Between the buy-in level of 825 and the sell-out level of 1350 she has secured a profit of almost 64% – all of which she would have lost in the course of the following year.

Figure 26: Perfect Investment – S&P 500 Index

With the index level now back to, or even below, the level at which she invested originally, she now has the opportunity of repeating the exercise. But this time around she has a larger investment fund of $164,000 vs. the original $100,000.

This example has demonstrated the use of mental stops in the context of a long-term (multi-year, or beyond) investment in an index-tracking mutual fund. There is nothing inherent in this scenario that prevents it from being implemented using an exchange traded fund (ETF) or a rolling spread bet; in both cases with the benefit of automated stops.

In anyone's book, Debbie would be considered to be an investor rather than a trader. She really never wanted to get stopped out and her intention all along was to Long Term Buy and Hold (LTBH), but crucially not to Long Term Buy and Forget (LTBF). Investment purists might bemoan the fact that she has practised *market timing*, and – as they know – it is impossible to time the market. And yet, Debbie's $164,000 fund vs. their $100,000 fund (back to where they started) says that it is possible.

Alternative scenario

In this example, and the other perfect trade examples we can, of course conceive alternative scenarios in which things play out differently. The important thing to understand is not that success was achieved, but how the success was achieved. Applying stop orders in the same way should lead to success under other market conditions, albeit in the form of a different scenario.

In Debbie's case you might wonder what would have happened if she had concluded that the market had bottomed out after the big dip three-quarters of the way through 2001. She would have bought in at 1000, and on the subsequent dip in early 2002 would have noted a mental stop order at an appropriate level below this support level – as it happens, at the break-even point of 1000. By mid-2002 she would have been disciplined enough to sell out at this level, she would have avoided further losses in that year, and she would have been free to buy in again in 2003 as per the original scenario.

Author's Perfect Trading Results

As preparation for this book, and of course also to make some money, I ran a portfolio of rolling spread bets on UK, European and USA stocks in the period 02 March 2009 to 4 May 2009. This example is important because it represents a real traded portfolio with a real risk of loss; not merely paper trading, nor back testing designed to find a period over which the techniques just happened to work.

This real-life example demonstrates the possibility (and possibility only) of using stop orders and position sizing combined with leverage and pyramiding to generate outsize returns *during a bull run.*

As of week ending 02 March 2009 (the start of the trial run) my spread betting account showed Net Equity (the amount that could be realised and withdrawn if any open positions were closed) of just £288.02. Don't laugh at this ridiculously small starting capital before I tell you that by week ending 11 May 2009 this had grown to Net Equity of £6815.69, an increase of more than 2200%, in the space of only ten weeks; with no additional cash deposits having been made along the way. It just goes to show that with the benefits of leverage, combined with sound risk management using stop orders, it is possible to make a worthwhile sum from virtually nothing.

The progress of this spread betting portfolio over the course of the ten weeks is given in the following table.

The eagle-eyed amongst you will notice that all of these week-ending dates fall on a Monday. Don't ask me why, but this particular spread betting firm issues weekly statements as at 22:00 (10pm) every Monday.

Week Ending	Net Equity	£1 Bets Open	% Increase on the Week	Cumulative % Increase
02 March 2009	£288.02	15		
09 March 2009	£341.93	20	18.72%	181.72%
16 March 2009	£810.63	16	137.07%	81.45%
23 March 2009	£1393.08	24	71.85%	383.67%
30 March 2009	£1031.22	32	-25.98%	258.04%
06 April 2009	£2311.19	40	124.12%	702.44%
13 April 2009	£3227.98	47	39.67%	1020.75%
20 April 2009	£3326.25	58	3.04%	1054.87%
27 April 2009	£4062.66	76	22.14%	1310.55%
04 May 2009	£5709.49	82	40.54%	1882.32%
11 May 2009	£6815.69	96	19.37%	2266.39%

It wasn't all plain sailing. As you can see, the net equity figure actually fell by about 25% between w/e 23 March 2009 and w/e 30 March 2009, but at this point the portfolio was still showing a cumulative (i.e. compounded) return of 258% over the four weeks.

The third column of this table shows the total number of £1 spread bets that remained open at the end of each week. As the net equity increased, and my stops were gradually raised, more notional funds were released thereby allowing me to place more rolling bets – without having to introduce any more cash funds. By the time 96 x £1 spread bets were open, this does not mean that positions were held in 96 different stocks. Some existing positions will have been added to; such that an open £3-per-point spread bet on Barclays Bank (for example) is counted as three separate £1-per-point spread bets.

The final net equity value of £6815.69 is the maximum value that I could have realised by closing all open positions manually at that time, but more likely is that I would wait for those positions to get stopped out of their own accord. Note that the main purpose of placing and then raising my stop levels in this trial was not to stop a loss, nor in fact to secure a profit, but to free up additional trading funds for the rapid pyramiding of my positions. It's not for the faint-hearted, but it demonstrates a role for stop orders beyond the traditional stop-loss role.

Although I stopped the clock officially at ten weeks so as to meet the initial manuscript deadline for this book, you will no doubt be keen to hear how it went in the subsequent weeks. After a significant market correction, which by week 19 reduced the total portfolio value to £4220 (or a 1434% increase since the start, still not bad), at 26 weeks the net equity figure had increased to a new high of £9284.20. I closed out all my open positions for a total return of 3123% over six months.

I have included these details so as to demonstrate, with real-life evidence, that a trend-following position-trading system that utilises stop orders as a mechanism for freeing up funds for pyramiding can be very effective when done correctly under favourable market conditions. But I offer no assurances whatsoever that it will work for you, or even me, in the future under different market conditions. The *period in question was a very exceptional time*: an early stage bull market in which a simple buy-and-hold strategy with the same stocks may well have been effective, but not *as* effective. The buy-and-holder could not have freed up additional risk capital – notionally in a regular brokerage account, or actually in a spread betting account – through the application of stop orders. He would therefore not have been able to pyramid his position(s) in this way.

How was it done?

You may be interested to learn about the trading rules that I used in order to effect this impressive performance. They were:

1.   Place a bet on a potential recovery stock that had fallen massively, was priced low, and which I thought had now bottomed out; with a **stop loss order** below the stock's lowest historic price, or with no stop order at all if I could stand the loss associated with a total wipe-out.

2.   When the price has risen, corrected, and then risen again so as to establish a new support level, raise the **stop order to sell** at a safe distance below the support level.

3.   With any new funds available as a result of the increased net equity and raised stop(s), repeat from step 1.

Thus in each daily cycle I raised the stop levels of any existing open positions and I invested any increased trading funds in the same stock or other stocks that I found to be compelling. This is the trading technique known as *pyramiding*.

In Figure 27, I demonstrate the pyramiding technique in the context of a single stock. The price history is for Barclays Bank, which was one of the constituents of my portfolio, but that's not really important. The pyramiding technique can be applied to any stock, index, commodity, currency or any other tradable instrument.

The sequence of events is as follows:

1.   I buy at 75 and place no stop order, therefore my secured profit is -75 (i.e. a potential loss).

2.   When the price corrects I buy at 150 and move my stop (on both positions) to 125. The secured profit on my original position is now 50 (calculated as 125-75) and the secured profit on my new position is -25 (calculated as 125-150), giving an overall secured profit (or new risk capital) of 25.

3. When the price corrects again I buy at 200 and move my stop (on all my positions) to 175. My overall secured profit – which you can work out for yourself – is now 100.

4. When the price corrects again I buy at 250 and move my stop (on all my positions) to 225. My overall secured profit – which you can work out for yourself – is now 225.

Figure 27: Pyramiding example – Barclays Bank

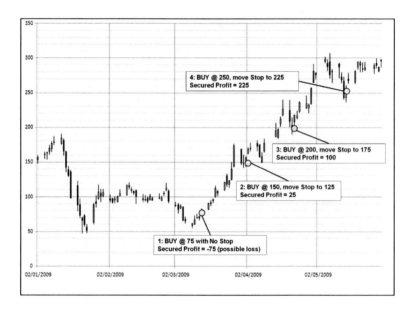

Now, if you are interested in what my other chosen hot stocks were, I'll tell you. But it won't do you any good except as something for you to analyse historically. By the time you read this, you will surely have missed the boat with these particular stocks. But it doesn't matter. Analysing and picking good stocks (or commodities, or whatever) at the right time will only help to tip the probability of success in your favour. It is your stop-based trading system that will keep you in the game long enough to realise the true potential of your investments.

In his book *The Way to Trade*, John Piper demonstrates why money management (which is what my use of stop orders is really all about) is far more important than stock analysis. As he puts it:

Your entry cannot wipe you out – but the way you exit can.

If you still want to know what my stellar stocks were, I can tell you that the ones with positions still open at the end of the experiment were:

AIG (American International Group), Allied Irish Banks, American Express, Aviva, Bank Of Ireland, Barclays, Barratt Development, British Airways, Brixton plc, BT Group, Citigroup, Commerzbank, Cookson Group, Crocs, Debenhams, DSG International, E*TRADE Financial Corp, Enterprise Inns, Ferrexpo, Fifth Third Bankcorp, Fortis, Friends Provident, Inchcape, ITV, Kazakhmys, Liberty International, Lloyds Banking Group, Minerva, Old Mutual, Paragon Group, Punch Taverns, Rank, RBS Group, Savills, Segro plc, Sports Direct, St James Place, St Modwen, Taylor Wimpey, Trinity Mirror, UK Coal, Wolseley, and Workspace Group.

A few other stocks will have been sold along the way, most likely at a profit, or otherwise at a small loss. And remember that the ongoing positions in all of these stocks have been established from an initial trading equity of less than £300 (about $450). At the end of the experiment these positions could have had further to go (and I can now tell you with the benefit of hindsight that they did have much further to go).

A note about diversification

You will notice that by the end of this trial, positions were held in 43 different stocks, which represents a fair spreading of risk. And yet these positions represent only a handful of market sectors, predominantly finance and real estate with a sprinkling of other stocks that also performed very poorly during the 2007-2008 crisis and subsequent recession. In this respect, the portfolio is not very diverse.

You might therefore wonder about my attitude to diversification.

I agree with the sentiment expressed by George Soros that "diversification is for the birds". What's the point in holding a balanced portfolio of different asset classes (equities, bonds, cash, property, and so on) or a balanced portfolio of different stock sectors such that when one half of the portfolio goes up, the other half goes down to cancel out the gains? To me, that sounds like a recipe for standing still or at best achieving exactly average returns.

I also agree with Warren Buffett's quote – which was originally Mark Twain's, I think – that it's better to "put all your eggs in one basket, and watch the basket very carefully". Whether or not Buffet actually uses them, and I assume he doesn't, **stop orders** are a very effective way of watching your basket very carefully. But they are not foolproof, unless guaranteed. So for me, diversification provides protection against *the only significant risk that I need to worry about*: the risk that a stop order on a single security may not execute as expected, or at all, thus wiping me out.

Otherwise, diversification allows me to bet on several horses in the same race, safe in the knowledge that my **(trailing) stop orders** will let me ride the best runners to the end of the race. But these are still only the best runners out of the limited number of horses that I think have the best chance at the start. There's no point diversifying across all the horses – including the lame mares – at the beginning of the race; and if you know anything at all about horse racing, you'll know that placing a bet on every single horse in a race assures you a net profit of zero (or worse).

That's not what you said in your earlier book!

Those of you who have read my earlier book *DON'T LOSE MONEY! (in the Stock Markets)*, which, like this book, was also on the subject of good money management, will wonder why I have turned to stock picking in my demonstration portfolio. Didn't I say in the previous book that I was an index investor?

Well, at that time, with the market at a historic high, there simply weren't any obvious opportunities to seek out stocks that could be potential ten-baggers. Preservation of capital was more important than the acquisition of additional capital. But that all changed with the 2007-2008 financial crisis that relegated even the most blue-chip stocks to penny-share status, and therefore ripe for recovery. As John Maynard Keynes is reported as saying:

> *When the facts change sir, I change my mind! What do you do?*

But the prior advice still stands for those of you who have already amassed a large fortune through regular work, who want to protect it at all costs, and who want to 'play the markets' without losing your shirt. In those cases, diversification through index investing may be a very good thing, but – as expressed in the original book – diversification is insufficient in itself to protect you from the once-in-a-generation black swan events that bring the whole market down.

The only thing that can protect you, apart from advanced hedging techniques, is the stop order.

13

Imperfect Trades

As impressive as the performance outlined at the end of the previous chapter is, you should treat it with a degree of scepticism. The results I presented are absolutely true, and for the record were replicated in a second spread betting portfolio run simultaneously, but as far as you know I might be telling the truth – but not the whole truth. I might, for example, have run up huge losses in the run up to the selective time period I reported on.

This is why league tables of mutual funds and other investments are somewhat suspect; the marketing men shout about the investments that performed well, for the periods that they performed well, and let the unsuccessful investments die quietly without much fanfare. This is also why you should beware those trading and investment books that tell you only about the successes and not the failures.

In this chapter I aim to redress the balance of this book, by drawing your attention to the things that can – and do – go wrong when using stop orders. Understanding the failures is just as important as, and maybe even more important than, revelling in the excitement of the successes.

But don't be disheartened by these mini case studies. Many of the world's greatest traders and investors made significant losses in their early days, whilst perfecting their approaches. They regard their early losses as merely the cost of their trading education, as their attendance fees at the Investment School of Hard Knocks. The trick is to always stay in the game, and to not get wiped out before you graduate with your first class honours in trading. Stop orders help you to stay in the game. And when utilised correctly to cut your losses and run your profits, it is possible to come out with a net profit even if you have more failed trades than successful ones.

> *Note*: Traders make losses all the time, because admitting to a small loss and crystallising the loss is almost always better than ignoring it and leaving it to grow. So while the number of losses will not necessarily decrease as your trading improves, the effect of those losses certainly should.

You will make your own mistakes, and will learn more from them than I could ever teach you, but I hope that these scenarios will help to reduce the inevitable costs of your trading education at least a little. Of course, mistakes are only beneficial if you learn something from them, so I supplement these imperfect trading scenarios with some guidance on what could be done better next time around.

Imperfect Day Trade

Sally is a day trader. Her imperfect day trade is illustrated in Figure 28.

On Friday 17 April, Sally buys Bank of America at a level of 10.3 expecting the price to go up, and sets a tight stop loss at 10.1 to get out if wrong. The price rises for the rest of the day and she does not close the position at the end of the day. Since the position is held overnight – indeed, over a weekend – Sally should not be surprised to see that the price has gapped when the market next opens. The position is closed automatically; not at the stop level of 10.1 but at the gapped-down price of 9.5.

Figure 28: Imperfect Day Trade – Bank of America

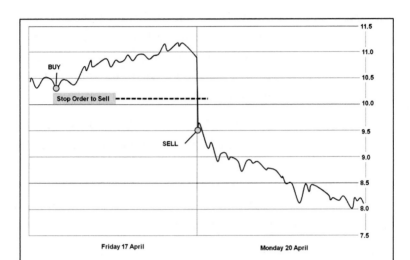

To some extent, the stop order has done its job of protecting against further losses as the price continues to trend downwards. But I still consider this to be an unsuccessful use of a stop order because the trader has lost 0.8 points (an 8% fall) and could have lost much more if the price had gapped down further; in contrast she could have banked a profit of 0.5 points (about 5%) by simply closing out the position at the end of the day – as any good day trader should. If the stop order had triggered during the first day, or had been *guaranteed* over the weekend, Sally's expected maximum loss could have been limited to 0.2 points.

This example demonstrates the danger of leaving a position open with a tight stop order overnight or over a weekend, when gaps are most likely to occur.

Imperfect Swing Trade

Jim is a swing trader. His imperfect swing trade is illustrated in Figure 29.

Mid-morning on 7 April 2009 Jim notices that the USD/CAD spot price has peaked twice just above the 1.245 level and troughed twice at around the 1.236 level. He plans to benefit from price swings within this trading range by selling short when the price rises to 1.244 and buying net long when the price falls to 1.238.

First he places a **limit order to sell** at 1.244, with a **stop loss order to buy** at 1.248 (in case he is wrong). It turns out that he is wrong, and shortly after the limit order executes the stop loss order also executes, thus creating a 4 point loss. Then it turns out that he was right after all, and so he misses out on the subsequent downswing through which he had planned to capture a profit of 6 points.

Not to worry. He missed the downswing, but he won't miss the next upswing thanks to his **limit order to buy** at 1.238 (with a **stop loss order sell** at 1.234 in case he is wrong). Once again, he is wrong, and his stop loss order executes shortly after his limit order for another loss of 4 points.

In this scenario Jim has suffered from the widening of the trading range, as can be seen clearly in the chart. So while the price has swung above and below a well-defined midpoint as expected, the upswings and downswings have become more exaggerated in each iteration; each time not breaking into a significant uptrend or downtrend but triggering the stop orders that were placed as protection against such trends developing.

Figure 29: Imperfect swing trade – USD/CAD

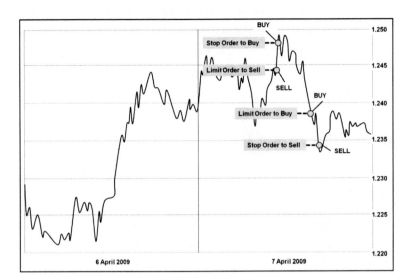

The question arises as to what Jim could do to avoid this situation; which turns out to be not much actually. There is no way that Jim can know in advance that a price advance or decline to his stop levels merely signifies a widening of the trading range rather than the establishment of a new trend. Maybe he should just accept the resulting whipsaw losses as a cost of doing (trading) business, and be confident in the knowledge that his stop orders would have protected him from significant losses in the case that the price did break out from the trading range as a precursor to a new trend.

It is possible, though, to make some general observations about Jim's trading behaviour:

- Since Jim is clearly not 'in tune' with the market, he may be wise to simply stay out for a while rather than risk over-trading by attempting to get even with the market.

- It appears that Jim is a day trader in swing trader's clothing, as he is trying to catch very minor swings within a single trading day; those swings perhaps representing market noise rather than important movements. He should re-evaluate his trading style and look to benefit from bigger swings over a longer time period.

Imperfect Position Trade

Bob is a position trader. His imperfect position trade is illustrated in Figure 30.

In mid-January 2009 Bob seizes the opportunity to buy shares in Barclays Bank at a price of 60p, some 92.5% from this stock's peak price in 2007. Since the price could fall further, even by a significant amount in percentage terms, before it rises, he decides not to place an initial stop loss order that could easily be triggered. Don't worry: he has sized his position so as to be comfortable with a total wipe-out on this stock, even though he considers this to be most unlikely. And he considers the potential ten-bagging upside to be a fair trade-off against the potential one-bagging downside.

The price does indeed fall slightly before it rises, but then rises rapidly back up to and beyond his original purchase price. At this point he sets a **stop order** to trail at 60 points below the prevailing price. Initially this is equivalent to his original idea of having no stop order, and the stop level rises in line with the rising price to reach a level of 55 (approaching break-even) when the price peaks at 115 in late January.

So far so good as the price stabilises in a trading range significantly above the stop level – until the price subsequently falls, triggers the stop order, and closes out the position for a small loss of 5 points. On the one hand, the **trailing stop order** has done its job by stopping Bob out not far below his break-even point. But at this point in early

March, Bob now faces a dilemma as to whether to re-establish the position that has just been sold out, which would incur an additional small loss resulting from transaction charges and the bid-ask spread.

It turns out that re-establishing the position – which undermines the point of the **stop order** in the first place – would be the right thing to do, but we can only know this for sure with the benefit of our perfect hindsight.

Figure 30: Imperfect Position Trade – Barclays Bank

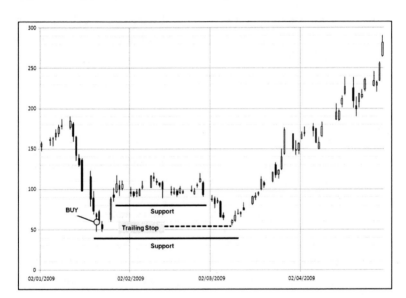

So the question is, how could Bob have worked this trade more effectively?

I can suggest three things that he could have done differently:

- He could have not established his long position at all until he had witnessed the double-bottom chart pattern that became apparent in early March, this pattern defining a support level at 40.

- He could have foregone the application of a trailing stop, instead relying on the courage of his initial convictions that no stop was necessary because his position size was manageable. He could always have introduced a **stop order** later on, when he could do so at a level at or above the original purchase price.

- He could have forgone the application of a **stop order** until he witnessed the interim support level at 80 during February; at which point a tighter stop at this level would have secured a profit of 20 points versus his realised loss of 5 points.

Only with hindsight could Bob have discovered which of those strategies would have been most effective – but the fact is that any one of those strategies would have been more effective than the approach he took in reality.

Imperfect Investment

This one is not a failure to utilise stop orders effectively, but rather a failure due to not using them at all.

Debbie is an investor and her imperfect investment is illustrated in Figure 31.

In 1999 Debbie inherited a sum of money and was advised by a financial adviser that over the long term stocks always outperformed cash deposits. She was also advised that attempting to time the market was futile and that "time in the market" was all that mattered. And so, with ten years to run until retirement, Debbie deposited all of her $100,000 inheritance in an index tracking fund; and she waited and she watched. Figure 31 shows what happened.

(For the moment, ignore the horizontal lines labelled Support and Resistance.)

Notice how Debbie's initial investment had fallen by about 30% by 2002. Not a good start but, hey, this is meant to be a long-term investment. And indeed, her investment then rose steadily until 2007 to become worth about $140,000 plus the value of any dividends along the way. Then it all went wrong. The Dow Jones index fell as a result of the international credit crisis, and by 2009 Debbie's capital (ignoring dividends) had fallen to a low point of -35%, to subsequently rebound slightly and end the ten-year period with a capital loss of about 15%.

Not only is a return of -15% over ten years (ignoring dividends) a complete disaster for Debbie's imminent retirement plans, but also it would have been something of an emotional roller-coaster along the way; a roller-coaster that would have most likely caused Debbie to withdraw from her investment in desperation at the most inopportune time.

So this was Debbie's reward for 'investing wisely' and following the financial advisor's advice to *blindly buy and hold*.

Figure 31: Imperfect Investment – Dow Jones Industrial Average (DJI) Index

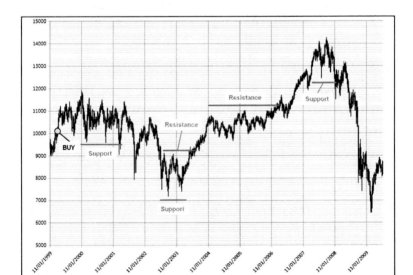

The point about this tale is that it demonstrates how Debbie was at the mercy of big swings in the market, when with some rudimentary market timing – only three or four trades over the ten year period – she could in fact have benefitted from those market swings. All thanks to stop orders.

A smarter investor named Denise is not so religious about blindly buying and holding. By identifying key support and resistance levels (suggested by the additional horizontal lines that I told you to ignore previously), and by applying appropriate position sizing with an element of market timing using stop orders, she achieved a positive return over the same ten-year period. She sold whenever the price crossed a key support level (using a **stop order to sell**) and bought when the price crossed a key resistance level (using a **stop order to buy**). Her trading transcript is as follows:

1. Funds available at start = $100,000.

2. Invest $50,000 at 10,000 in 1999.

3. Close out the position when the price falls below the support level of 9500 in 2001, leaving $47,500 plus the uninvested $50,000 = $97,500.

4. Invest $50,000 when the price rises above the resistance level of 9200 in 2003, with a **stop loss order** at the support level of 7000.

5. Invest the balance of $47,500 when the price rises above the resistance level of 11200 in 2006, with a stop loss order (for both of the positions) at the support level of 9500.

6. Sell out both positions when the price falls below the higher support level (and higher stop level) of 12,200 at the end of 2007; for a 33% capital increase on the $50,000 position and a 9% increase on the $47,500 position.

Denise's end result is a capital fund of $118,000 after ten years, which is adequate but not spectacular in absolute terms; but which is spectacular when compared with Debbie's capital loss of 15% over the same period.

At this point, the original financial advisor should shout up that Debbie's "time in the market" would have enabled her to collect additional dividend income along the way. And Denise should counter that she too was "in the market" for about half the time (hence collecting dividends) and in the meantime her uninvested funds would have been earning interest on deposit. Her maximum drawdown (or loss) during the ten years was $2,500 (only 2.5% of her initial funds), hence her emotional roller-coaster was a much gentler ride than Debbie's!

Author's "Imperfect Trade" Example – Barclays Bank

As you read the following mini case study you may well experience some déjà vu, as it is reminiscent of Bob's imperfect day trade described earlier. In fact, the same price history for the same stock (Barclays Bank) shown in Figure 30 may help you to visualise this scenario – as long as you ignore Bob's placements of stops. Although this example utilises the same price history for the same stock over the same time period, this is my (the author's) real-life imperfect trade rather than Bob's hypothetical trade. And whereas Bob attempted to utilise a **trailing stop order** at a fixed distance, I attempt to adjust my stop level manually.

I had been following Barclays Bank and other banking stocks as their prices declined in 2008, establishing small exploratory positions each time I thought they had bottomed out. This is called 'bottom fishing'. I set a stop-loss order on each exploratory trade, which resulted in a small but manageable loss each time the price fell further.

On 21 January 2009, I placed a £1-per-point spread bet on Barclays Bank at 62p. Not the exact bottom, which was about 50p, but a price at which I was happy to not place a stop-loss order. At this low price my maximum loss in the unlikely case of a total wipe-out could be limited to £62, while my maximum gain (if the stock ever returned to its all-time high of around 800p) could be approximately £700. With a potential upside of almost 12x the potential downside, this appeared to be a worthwhile speculation.

You can figure out for yourself what the downside and upside potential would be for a bigger £10 spread bet or a sizable investment in the equity itself, but my preference was to limit the risk initially through position sizing (not staking too much) rather than by setting a tight **stop loss order**.

On 26 January the Barclays chairman, Marcus Agius, and chief executive, John Varley, wrote an open letter to investors stating that the yet-to-be-reported pre-tax profits would be well ahead of the £5.3bn estimate – which sent the shares soaring by more than 73% percent the next day. I wasn't tempted to sell out for a big profit, nor to set a tight stop-loss to protect my notional big profit, because I was now in this position for as long as possible. But I did apply a **stop loss order** at my original buy-in price of 62p, so as to hopefully eliminate any potential loss – providing the stop-loss was to execute at the specified price. As I thought, this stock had truly bottomed out in the previous week and I never expected this order to actually trigger at any point.

In the period from 28 January to 28 February, the Barclays Bank share price oscillated in a well-defined range from 83p (a support level) to 120p (a resistance level). This raised the possibility of raising the **stop loss order** to 80p, thus assuring a profit of 18 points (29%). But I didn't do it.

To cut a long story short, the price subsequently fell back to my stop level of 62p and sold me out for zero profit on 9 March. Ironically, this price level formed the second bottom of a classic 'double bottom' chart pattern, and the price rose thereafter more-or-less continuously to sit at around 300p (£3) as of 5 May 2009. Recognising the double-bottom for what it was, and convinced that my original reasoning was sound, I bought in again soon after my stop loss order had been triggered, and therefore I did benefit from the subsequent sustained rise. The day was saved.

So, did I regard my original trade as a failure?

Not really, and you should remember that this chapter is about *imperfect trades* rather than necessarily *failed trades*. My original trade could not be classed as a total failure because the **stop loss order** did its job of protecting me from a potential loss. But the trade wasn't perfect, and, on the face of it, it might have been improved by:

1. Adjusting the **stop order** to 80 when the higher support level had been identified; thus assuring *some* profit with the risk of over-trading and the risk of closing the position prematurely.

2. Not applying a **stop order** at all, and relying on my limited position size until such time as I could place a stop order that would secure a decent profit with little risk of being stopped out.

3. Adjusting the original stop loss order to no higher than the original observed low point of 50p, rather than prematurely trying to break-even at 62p.

Although it all worked out for me in the end, because I bought in again at just the right time, I could have saved myself the hassle of having to time and place a second trade by taking the second or third course of action in the preceding list – my preference being the third course of action. In other words, beware the premature break-even stop which looks attractive in theory but which in practice may simply be a way of crystallising a profit (albeit zero) too soon.

Note that the first course of action in my list, although securing a profit, would only secure a small profit due to the small position size; and it would still have left me with the problem of whether – and when – to re-enter the position. Again, beware of securing a profit too soon.

14

When to Hold and When to Fold

The superstitious amongst you must have thought it very apt that the previous chapter on imperfect trades was numbered unlucky 13; but superstition has no place in the trader's mindset. When entering the trading room we need to leave superstition at the door along with human emotions such as fear, greed and – most of all – blind optimism.

Investors who buy and blindly hold for the long term live by optimism alone; optimism that their obviously falling stocks will live to rise again, and will keep rising until (by sheer luck) they peak at just the right time to cash-in for retirement. It might just happen, but much more likely is that it won't. And it's a long time to wait in order to discover that your optimism was misplaced.

I once read a quote (I don't remember the source) which I paraphrase as:

Optimism is hoping for the best whereas confidence is knowing how to handle the worst.

Stop orders give us the confidence that we can handle the worst. By using stop orders effectively we can harness the power of good luck while escaping the ravages of bad luck. It's all a matter of knowing "when to hold and when to fold".

When to Hold and When to Fold

Many traders and authors have observed that trading is much like playing gambling games such as poker.

Just as there are successful traders, there are professional poker players who make money consistently over the long term. Not because they can predict the flow of cards but because they practice sound risk management. With only average luck (50% success rate) or even less, it is still possible to come out with a net profit providing your wins are bigger than your losses; providing you know when to hold (for the bigger pot) and when to fold (take your small loss and live to play again).

Poker players know when to "hold 'em" and when to "fold 'em", just as your stop orders tell you when to keep holding positions and when to fold (exit) those positions.

Good poker players also practice good money management by knowing when to bet the farm and when not (usually not) – possibly in accordance with the Kelly Formula that we looked at in Chapter 11. They know about position sizing, and the important interplay between the size of bet and the decision to hold or fold.

Finally, they understand human psychology. They know when other players are fearful or greedy, and they play accordingly. As Warren Buffett says:

> Be greedy when others are fearful, and fearful when others are greedy.

It may be no surprise to learn that many good traders are also good poker players. Both disciplines require a good understanding of when to hold and when to fold, and that's what this book is really about: *risk management*. Both disciplines also require a good understanding of how much to risk when raising the ante; another key theme of this book, which went under the names *position sizing* and *money management*.

Traders who know When to Hold and When to Fold

When taking advice, it is always a good idea to seek a second opinion. Rather than expect you to take only my word for it in this book, I thought it would be useful to relay the thoughts of other successful contemporary traders who incorporate stop orders as an integral part of their trading strategies; people who know when to hold and when to fold.

Malcolm Pryor

Malcolm Pryor is a member of the Society of Technical Analysts in the UK and has been designated a Certified Financial Technician by the International Federation of Technical Analysts. He is the best-selling author of *The Financial Spread Betting Handbook* and other books on trading and investment, and editor of Spread Betting Central (www.spreadbettingcentral.co.uk). Given my comparison between trading and card games above, it should be no surprise that Malcolm holds the rank of Grandmaster at the card game bridge.

Here are some top tips for using stop orders, kindly contributed to this book by Malcolm. You will find them reassuringly consistent with my own guidance in this book, despite the fact that no prior collusion has taken place (honest!).

1) Many traders and investors tend to focus mainly on entries; but the reality is that your entry is probably one of the least important parts of your methodology. Exits, bet size and psychology are all much more important to success.

2) Successful traders and investors generally work out where they will get out if it goes against them before they put on a position.

3) The amount risked on a position should be directly related to a) where your stop is going to be placed and b) how much per position you are prepared to risk.

4) There are a huge range of techniques for managing stops once in a position, and the techniques chosen will alter the characteristics of a series of trades or investments. In addition to the initial protective stop, a trailing stop can be used to maintain a position while protecting profits and allowing the opportunity for profits to run; whereas the technique of exiting at a target will bag a profit at a predetermined reward level while surrendering the opportunity for further gains. Both these two techniques have merit in certain situations.

5) The actual exit techniques used need to be matched to the trading style, risk preferences, and objectives of the trader or investor.

6) In the UK, spread betting platforms mostly have a reasonably sophisticated selection of order facilities including stop orders both to enter and exit, and the extremely useful OCO (One Cancels Other) orders and contingent orders (which usually only get placed if a new trade is entered). The same applies to CFD (Contracts for Difference) platforms.

7) Successful spread bettors generally have an excellent working knowledge of the order types available on the platforms they use.

8) Some people prefer to have a mental stop, i.e. know where they will exit, but not place a stop formally on the platform they use. This only works if the individual has the discipline to obey the stop when the relevant price is hit.

Nick McDonald

Nick left his 9-5 job within 3 months of discovering technical analysis and is now an independent, full-time trader. In addition to being a highly talented trader, Nick is also a well respected trading mentor and founded 'Trade With Precision' (www.tradewithprecision.com) to teach aspiring traders his unique approach to trading with technical analysis.

Nick contributed the following text under the title "Tight Stops – The Conservative Approach". In contrast to my own use of stop orders for *position trading*, Nick's contribution illustrates how tighter stop orders work for him in his short-term trading approach:

> I have met many self-proclaimed 'conservative' traders who think that the use of wide stops is what makes their trading conservative. They state that this approach means their stop is "less likely to be hit" and therefore it is a "sensible, more cautious approach". They are correct on one thing, the stop is less likely to be hit. The stop, however, is just one factor in profitable trading and conservative does not always equal profitable. This is often conservative to the point of being detrimental to trading success!
>
> A tight versus a wide stop can of course be quite different across a range of timeframes and products; however, let's compare two scenarios on a share that's trading at, say, 1500. Let's call an aggressive, tight stop on this 30 points and a conservative, wide stop, 120 points. Also, let's assume the widely agreed approach that you must have reward to risk in your favour: i.e. if you risk \$1, you must stand to make at least \$1 or more; a 1:1 reward to risk ratio or greater.

The Conservative Trader

Will risk 120 points and therefore must make 120 points to be sufficiently profitable to justify taking the trade and achieve the 1:1 ratio. This requires an 8% move in the underlying. It is a risk of $1 to make $1.

The Good Trader

Will also see that there is room for a 120 point move into profit but will only execute the trade if a precise moment presents itself where he can have a well placed stop just 30 points away. Note: The Good Trader does not just have a tight stop for the sake of it, he or she waits only for the correct trades that actually justify it. There will be multiple technical factors protecting the stop loss from been hit in the form of support and resistance levels. There are minimal to no technical factors stopping the target from been hit. To be sufficiently profitable, the good trader only needs to move 30 points into profit to justify the trade, a 2% move in the underlying. If the trade does go on to move 120 points as predicted, the good trader is up 4 times what the Conservative Trader is up. It is a risk of $1 to make between $1 and $4.

Which is more conservative? Trying to predict an 8% move or a 2% move? The Good Trader profits in either scenario.

The success of my trading has been built on the exact opposite philosophy to wide stops – tight targets are actually what is conservative but only in the situation where the tight stop too is justified. The Good Trader waits patiently for these opportunities. I would much sooner have a conservative target that makes me money than a conservative stop that loses it!

A trader should not assess whether a stop is likely to be hit soon, rather, what is more likely to be hit first: stop loss or

> target? A precision entry with a defined trading strategy, a
> technically protected stop loss and a target with no technical
> support or resistance stopping it from been hit is the approach
> that I recommend all traders work to adopt.

Mike Baghdady

Mike Baghdady began his career in New York as an apprentice to
Alan Shaw, widely considered to be the father of modern technical
analysis. Since then he has worked as a commodities trader, stock
trader, futures analyst, options trader and an instructor for both
foreign currency exchange and equities markets.

Mike's catchphrase

Trade What You See, Not What You Think

is the foundation of his industry-acclaimed strategy, which eliminates
the emotion and guesswork in trading. His London-based school,
Spyglass Trading Solutions (www.spyglasstrading.co.uk), teaches
traders to manage risk and exposure through a unique price action
system that provides his students with a quantifiable edge to increase
their probability of success.

Like Nick McDonald, Mike is a short-term trader. In this
contribution he reiterates the important relationship between stop
placement and position size, and he introduces the notion of another
kind of stop – the **time stop**:

> Every day, traders sit in front of their screens, staring at the
> charts wondering whether to buy or sell. As soon as they decide
> on a trade and before they place their order, they must study the
> charts and identify an exit point representing their line in the
> sand if the market moves against their position. If they do not
> see or settle on an exit point, they shouldn't enter into the trade!

These exit points are where we control our risk – we place our stops in order to exit out of a trade which is not going our way.

My Number One rule is: "Once I am in a hole, I must stop digging." I get out, and I never move my stop. Also, I never, ever place a Stop Limit Order to exit a losing position. I simply want to get out as soon as is possible.

As to deciding what is the right value of a stop, many traders decide to risk a fixed dollar amount for every trade, and settle on that amount based upon either their bank roll or risk tolerance. However, the volatility of the market and of the instrument we are trading is never constant, so the value of our stops must be calculated to reflect these conditions.

When volatility increases we need to widen our stops, but at the same time reduce the size of our new position; because if our monetary stop happens to be too tight in a slightly more volatile market, we will most probably be stopped out of what could have been a successful trade, only because our stop was too tight.

If the markets are quiet and we can identify an exit point on the chart that is close enough to allow us to use a tighter stop, we can choose the smaller stop and slightly increase our position size. The winning maxim in trading is "Minimise your risk and maximise your size", so long as our dollar risk on any position is about the same.

I determine the value of my exit stops on a technical basis, below what I perceive is a turning point on the price chart (and not just what I would perceive as support or resistance) because these price-turning points are clearly marked on the charts as where the markets have decided to change direction. I then calculate my stop location and position size from where the prices are at the moment of entering the trade, factoring in these market turning points.

Another type of a stop I use, which has proven its value over the years, is what I call the 'Time Stop'. This is a second additional stop that I mentally place after I have entered into a trade and placed my price stop.

If I enter into a trade and the market fails to move in my direction after a set period, this indicates to me that I'm on the wrong side of the market or that the market has entered into a sideways pattern or will move in the opposite direction. In either case, holding onto a position that's going nowhere would be a waste of both my mental capital and eventually my financial capital.

Usually, my Time Stops are between 5-6 times the time-frame I am trading, so if I'm trading off a 15-minute chart and my position does not start to make money within 60-90 minutes, I exercise my Time Stop and close the trade regardless.

Taking Emotion out of Trading

The whole point of knowing when to hold and when to fold, as a trader or professional gambler, is to take the emotion out of trading. You set a stop order at a rational level when you have a clear head, so that it executes automatically when you don't. Otherwise your trading decisions will be driven by the irrational emotions of greed and fear. As the old gambler's adage says:

Scared money never wins.

Key Points

- Successful traders are like professional poker players: they know how to benefit from a small edge over the long term by practising sound risk- and money- management.

- For many traders, stops orders are a central and indispensable feature of their trading strategies. While agreeing on the core principles, their specific uses of stop orders may differ slightly according to their chosen markets, timescales, strategies, and objectives.

- Take the emotion out of trading, because "Scared money never wins!"

15

Top Tips for Using Stop Orders

Whereas Part 1 of this book served as a reference guide to the types of stop orders, Part 2 has advised on best practice use of stop orders. This advice is summarised here for your convenience, as a list of top ten tips for using stop orders.

1. Use **stop orders** to *stop a loss* and **trailing stop orders** to *secure a profit without crystallising it*.

2. Use **trailing stop orders** to establish positions at a favourable price: to *buy low* (for long trades) and/or *sell high* (for short trades).

3. Use *tight stops* for day trading, *wide stops* for position trading and investment, and *protective stops* for swing trading.

4. Consider *support* and *resistance* levels as well as *volatility* when placing stops.

5. Beware *obvious* stop levels.

6. Use stop orders in conjunction with *position sizing*.

7. Consider **guaranteed stops, stops-with-limits,** and the temporary removal of stop orders as *protection against price gaps*.

8. Use manually-trailed stop orders as a *cure for over-trading* and *don't* try to *fully automate* your trading strategy using stop orders.

9. Spread bettors should understand the difference between a standalone **stop order** and a position-specific **stop loss order**.

10. Consider using stop orders as a mechanism for freeing up risk capital to *pyramid* positions.

And here is a bonus tip:

• Always *respect your stop orders*: in the heat of the moment, don't let the negative emotions of fear and greed override your stop order policy.

16

Conclusion: The Case For and Against Stop Orders

The usefulness and effectiveness of stop orders as a trading mechanism is a cause of some debate within the trading and investment communities. Some people swear by them, while some think that they do more harm than good.

In Curtis Faith's book *Way of the Turtle* he shows in one chapter how certain trend-following trading systems perform better when stop orders are not applied. And then in a later chapter he presents stop orders as nonetheless an indispensable trading mechanism. Don't worry, it's not a mistake – he knows what he is saying, and why he's saying it.

In this final chapter I present briefly the case against stop orders along with my indications of why I think the argument is flawed. And then I round off with my summary in favour of stop orders – in case you were in any doubt as to where I stand on this!

The Case Against Stop Orders

I was inspired to write this section by an article I read on the UK's Motley Fool website (www.fool.co.uk). The article in question was titled "Stop Losses Will Strangle Your Returns"[4].

The basic premise of the article is that stop orders can be dangerous and can erode your trading capital over time due to whipsaw losses. It's a fair point, but my argument would be that it's when stop orders are used naively that this may be true. Just as cars are not dangerous (only their drivers), stops orders are not dangerous in the hands of good traders. Or, to put it another way:

A poor workman always blames his tools.

While I consider the article to be logically flawed – after all, I have suggested throughout this book that stop orders allow you to *cut your losses* and *run your profits* so as to increase your trading capital rather than erode it – the article does do a good job of raising some important points including:

- The fact that stop orders are particularly useful to traders who use leverage, margin, gearing, or whatever else we choose to call it.

- The danger of attempting to quickly, and repeatedly, re-enter a position that you have been stopped out of – thereby courting whipsaw losses.

- The importance of position sizing as a risk reduction mechanism.

---

[4] http://www.fool.co.uk/news/investing/investing-strategy/2009/05/13/stop-losses-will-strangle-your-returns.aspx

What I *disagree* with are the implications that:

- Because stop orders are vital to leveraged traders, they are therefore of little or no use to non-leveraged long-only investors.

- Because ill-placed stop orders and compulsive over-trading leads to whipsaw losses, we should not even use well-placed stop orders that we respect (by not re-entering too soon) when they stop us out.

- Because position sizing offers an alternative risk management technique, we have no need for stop orders at all, even as a complementary technique.

The main case against stop orders in the cited article seems to be that they cause you to crystallise a loss that may in fact not turn out to be a loss if only you hold on for long enough. That sounds like blind optimism to me, and the question to ask ourselves is whether it's better to crystallise a 10% loss and move on to a better opportunity or to hold on for the possible 100% loss. And we shouldn't forget that a stop order can also be used to crystallise a profit, which a blind buy-and-hold approach can never do.

I recently discovered a more recent article[5] on the same website titled "The Reality Of Stop-Losses". A different author but the same underlying message that stop orders can do more harm than good – and with some real-life (but limited) evidence that they had.

I agree that in inexperienced hands stop orders can work against you. But I think this particular author has made at least two fundamental mistakes in his use of stop orders:

---

[5] www.fool.co.uk/news/investing/investing-strategy/2009/09/10/the-reality-of-stop-losses.aspx

First, his approach was to use stop orders to run losses and lock in profits, which of course is exactly opposite to the experienced trader's advice to "cut losses and let profits run". I quote:

> *Interestingly, I couldn't bring myself to set any stop-losses on those shares that haven't made any profits yet. Locking in a 10% loss didn't seem as appealing as locking in a 25% gain.*

Second, his automatic trailing of stop orders may have been too keen, and with no regard to established support levels or trading characteristics.

The Case For Stop Orders

As was shown theoretically in Part 1 and then practically in Part 2 of this book, stop orders can be used as an effective mechanism that allows you to "cut your losses and run your profits", which most if not all successful traders regard as the first rule of trading.

Stop orders are applicable whether you trade long or short, and they may be utilised over all trading timescales from short-term day trading to longer-term position trading and investing. While the way you utilise stop orders (Part 2 of the book) may depend on your trading or investment style, the basic mechanism is the same.

Although automated stop orders are not available on all tradable instruments via all brokers, the underlying concept may be useful even to mutual fund investors. And whereas not all brokers offer trailing stops, there is nothing to prevent you trailing them manually by adjusting the fixed stop-out level in line with the price trend.

When I ask traders the question "Why do you use stop orders?" the majority answer with, "to cut a loss" or, "to secure a profit". While I do both of those things, I also look at stop orders from a different angle: as a mechanism for freeing up funds for pyramiding, and as a cure for the ever-present threat of over-trading (because adjusting a stop order gives me something to do in the market without costing me a penny).

Above all, stop orders take the emotion out of trading decisions. By specifying in advance the conditions under which you will buy or sell, and by respecting those decisions without question when the time comes, you protect yourself from trading under pressure driven by the negative emotions of fear and greed.

In a nutshell:

> *Stop orders are the one essential weapon in the armoury of every trader, investor and spread bettor.*

And finally...

In this book I have made the case for stop orders by demonstrating what can go right when you use them correctly, and also what can go wrong if you use them incorrectly or not at all. I have tried to present a warts-and-all account, and in this respect I am not afraid to document my own less-than-perfect trades – one of which you encountered in Chapter 13. I'd like to end this chapter, and the book, telling one more story about the danger of *not using stop orders*.

Long-term investments

During 2007, the price of many banking and house-building stocks fell by 50%, and the stock market effectively put up a sign declaring *Half-Price Sale Now On!*

Who wouldn't go on a spending spree during such an unprecedented sale?

And so I did, by establishing a portfolio comprising stocks from the hardest-hit sectors. I was seduced by how much better value these stocks now were – not just in a relative sense (i.e. relative to their previous higher prices), but also in a more objective sense based on their forecast fundamentals.

> Beware making investment decisions based purely on simple fundamentals ratios, and in particular on the analysts' forecasts thereof. Not only are ratios like P/E and PEG too simplistic to be treated in isolation, but the estimates of *earnings* on which these ratios are based can be very wide of the mark in times of crisis. A too-good-to-be-true dividend yield can also be misleading, because a doubling of the apparent yield may be simply be a mathematical illusion resulting from a halving of the share price.

The value proposition was so great that I saw no need to put protective stop orders in place, and I had been clever enough – or so I thought – to diversify across several stocks, albeit several stocks from the same sectors. Like so many City professionals, I was wrong-footed by what would turn out to be an unremitting bear market.

When many of these half-price stocks had fallen by as much as 90%, one would think that they could fall no further. I bought additional stocks at the *90% Off Sale!*, again seeing no need for protective stop orders at those prices.

And that's when I discovered that even stocks that have fallen by 90% can easily fall by another 90%!

After all: the investors who purchased at 100p, who have seen the price of their shares fall by 90p to 10p, are unlikely to put up much of a fight to prevent those shares falling by a mere 9p more. So whereas those particular investors will have lost (on paper) a whopping 99% of their capital, even those investors who thought themselves clever (like me), who bought in at 10p, would have lost 90% of their capital with the shares now priced as penny stocks.

I'm not saying that my story played out exactly like this but, to cut a long story short, I ended up with a portfolio of 'long-term investments' that would surely recover...eventually. I don't feel too bad because this was not my only portfolio, and I was in the company of many esteemed City professionals who were also wrong-footed by these market conditions, but I do wish that in this case I had practiced what I have preached in this book and *cut my losses using stops*.

I should have known better, and I did. And now, so do you.

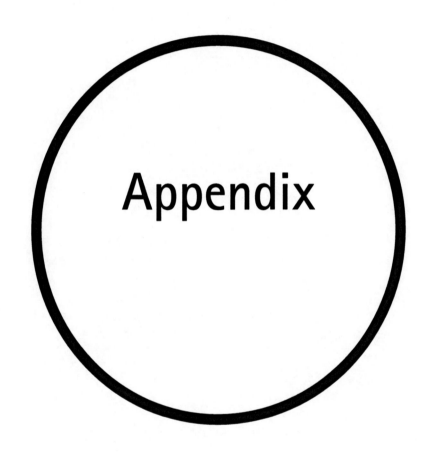

Appendix

Appendix

Stop Order Facilities by Broker

As mentioned throughout this book, spread betting firms and regular brokers typically offer a subset of the possible varieties of stop orders. Some offer **stop orders** but not **trailing stop orders**; some offer **automatic stop-loss orders,** and some don't. This appendix gives an indication – and an indication only – of the variations in brokers' support for stop orders.

> *Note*: The services offered by spread betting firms and brokers are liable to change at any time. If you are considering opening a new account, it is advisable to check the current situation regarding the services offered.

UK Spread Betting Firms

The following table gives an indication of the stop order facilities provided by the popular spread betting providers.

Note that in this table the presence of the word YES indicates that the firm's marketing literature indicated that relevant facility was provided at the time of writing this book. Absence of the word YES does not necessarily mean that the facility is definitely not provided, now or in the future, and so you should double-check with the platform provider.

Where spread betting providers use the same underlying trading platform (e.g. Party Markets / Barclays Stockbrokers / City Index), this does not necessarily mean that they offer exactly the same order types.

Name	Stop Orders	Trailing Stop Orders	Guaranteed Stop Orders	Stop-with-Limit Orders	Automatic Stop-Loss	URL
Barclays Stock-brokers	YES		YES		YES	www.stockbrokers.barclays.co.uk
City Index	YES		YES			www.cityindex.co.uk
E*TRADE	YES				YES	www.etradespreadbetting.com
ETX Capital	YES				YES (user preference)	www.etxcapital.co.uk
Financial Spreads	YES				YES	www.financialspreads.com
IG Index	YES	YES	YES (controlled-risk bets)			www.igindex.com
Paddy Power	YES				YES	www.paddypowertrader.com
Party Markets	YES		YES		YES (you can specify a default distance)	www.partymarkets.com
Shorts & Longs	YES		YES (free)		YES	www.shortsandlongs.com
SpreadEX	YES		YES			www.spreadex.com
TradeFair	YES				YES	www.tradefair.com

Most, if not all, spread betting firms allow stop orders to remain in force as *good for the day* (GFD), *good till cancelled* (GTC), or good until a specified time/date. Stop-loss orders that are attached to specific trades are always *good till cancelled*.

UK Stockbrokers

The following non-exhaustive table gives an indication of the stop order facilities provided by the popular stockbrokers in the UK on their regular brokerage, ISA, and SIPP accounts.

Although none of these brokers currently provides Guaranteed Stop Orders or Automatic Stop-Loss Orders, those columns are included for future updates and for consistency with the spread betting comparison table that follows.

Note that in this table the presence of the word YES indicates that the firm's marketing literature indicated that relevant facility was provided at the time of writing this book. Absence of the word YES does not necessarily mean that the facility is definitely not provided, now or in the future, and so you should double-check with the platform provider.

Name	Stop Orders	Trailing Stop Orders	Guaranteed Stop Orders	Stop-with-Limit Orders	Automatic Stop-Loss	URL
Barclays Stock-brokers	YES	YES		YES		www.stockbrokers.barclays.co.uk
Halifax Share Dealing	YES (Trade Plan)	YES (Price Locking)				www.halifax.co.uk/sharedealing
iWeb	YES (Trade Plan)	YES (Price Locking)				www.iweb-sharedealing.co.uk
Selftrade	YES	YES				www.selftrade.co.uk
TD Waterhouse	YES					www.tdwaterhouse.co.uk

Stockbrokers typically allow a stop order to remain in force for a specified number of days up to a maximum. For example, Barclays Stockbrokers allows orders to run for up to 30 business days, whereas Selftrade allow them to run for up to 90 business days.

Recommended Reading

Over the years I have read every trading and investment book that I could lay my hands on. The vast majority have fallen by the wayside because, to be frank, they just don't work; at least not for me. The following books have positively inspired my trading and they deserve pride of place in the library of the Investment School of Hard Knocks:

All About Market Timing, Leslie N. Masonson, McGraw-Hill, 2004

The Black Swan, Nassim Nicholas Taleb, Penguin, 2008

Extraordinary Popular Delusions and the Madness of Crowds, Charles Mackay, Harriman House, 2003

How I Made $2 Million in the Stock Market, Nicolas Darvas, Harriman House, 2007

Reminiscences of a Stock Operator, Edwin Lefévre, Wiley, 1994

Trade Your Way to Financial Freedom, Van K. Tharp, McGraw-Hill, 1998

Trend Following, Michael W. Covel, Prentice-Hall, 2006

The Way to Trade, John Piper, Harriman House, 2006

The Zurich Axioms, Max Gunther, Harriman House, 2005

Other Books by Tony Loton

Stock Fundamentals On Trial: Do Dividend Yield, P/E and PEG Really Work?

By Tony Loton, published by LOTONtech
(www.lotontech.com/money), 2008

Are high dividend yield, low P/E ratio, and low PEG ratio good indicators of future share price performance – as conventional wisdom would suggest? Did high yield stocks (the Yield Stars) perform much better than low yield stocks (the Yield Dogs) in recent years? Did low P/E stocks (the P/E Stars) perform much better than high P/E stocks (the P/E Dogs)? What about PEG Stars vs. PEG Dogs?

In this book I put company fundamentals on trial, using historic data and specially annotated charts as evidence. In weighing up the evidence I consider whether the buy-and-hold investor had any advantage over the market timer, and whether stock picking would have been more effective than index investing.

Financial Trading Patterns

By Tony Loton, published by LOTONtech
(www.lotontech.com/money), 2007

Do you know your limit order from your trailing stop order? For novice traders this book collates the order types provided by your stockbroker, and presents each one in the form of a standardised pattern that you can apply in your trading.

Do you combine your stockbroker's order types effectively in your trading or investment strategy? For intermediate traders this book presents standardised financial trading patterns that combine various order types, and which allow you to execute strategies such as:

- "Buy low, sell high"

- "Buy high, sell higher"

- "Cut your losses, let your profits run"

Each pattern comprises the pattern name, the motivation for the pattern, a pictorial success scenario, a pictorial failure scenario, and the application of the pattern in practice.

For a real-life perspective you will find details of the author's own use of trading patterns, as well as his back testing results.

DON'T LOSE MONEY! (in the Stock Markets)

By Tony Loton, published by LOTONtech (www.lotontech.com/money), 2007

If your investment falls by 50% you'll need a 100% rise just to get you back where you started. So when speculating in the stock markets, protecting the money you do have is just as important as making some more. This book is for you if you'd like to have a go at beating the system, but don't want to lose your shirt in the process. Topics covered include: index investing, market timing and trend following, stop loss orders, position sizing, and option spreads.

Index

Lightning Source UK Ltd.
Milton Keynes UK

171518UK00002B/31/P